The Discourse of Medicine:
Dialectics of Medical Interviews

D0148957

Language and Learning for Human Service Professions

A Series of Monographs
edited by
Cynthia Wallat, Florida State University
and
Judith Green, The Ohio State University

Volumes in the series include:

The Discourse of Medicine: Dialectics of Medical Interviews

ELLIOT G. MISHLER

Harvard Medical School and
Massachusetts Mental Health Center

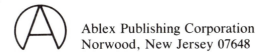

Ablex Publishing Corporation
Norwood, New Jersey 07648

Library of Congress Cataloging in Publication Data

Mishler, Elliot George, 1924–
    The discourse of medicine.

    (Language and learning for human service professions)
    "This . . . exchange between a patient and a physician is excerpted from the transcript of a tape recorded medical interview"—
    Bibliography: p.
    Includes indexes.
    1. Medical history taking. I. Title. II. Series.
[DNLM: 1. Communication. 2. Interviews—methods.
3. Physician—Patient Relations. W 62 M678d]
RC65.M57   1984   616.07'51   84-16832

ISBN 0-89391-276-X
ISBN 0-89391-277-8 (pbk.)

Ablex Publishing Corporation
355 Chestnut Street
Norwood, New Jersey 07648

Contents

For Nita
Co-maker and sharer of our lifeworld

Preface to the Series
Language and Learning for Human Service Professions

This series of monographs is intended to make the theories, methods, and findings of current research on language available to professional communities that provide human services. From a theoretical and practical point of view, focus on language as a social process means exploring how language is actually used in everyday life.

Communication between and among adults and children, professionals and clients, and teachers and students, as well as the effect of changing technology on communication in all these contexts, has become the object of study in disciplines as varied as anthropology, cognitive psychology, cognitive science, education, linguistics, social psychology, and sociology. The series provides a forum for this research analyzing talk in homes, communities, schools, and other institutional settings. The aim is to shed light on the crucial role of language and communication in human behavior.

The monographs in the series will focus on three main areas:

- Language and Social Relationships
- Language and Helping Professions
- Language and Classroom Settings

We hope that these books will provide rich and useful images of and information about how language is used.

Cynthia Wallat and Judith Green

Acknowledgments

I have benefited from the generosities of many friends and colleagues during the course of the study of medical interviews reported in this book. It is a pleasure to thank them for their help.

I wish, first, to express my appreciation to John Stoeckle and Howard Waitzkin who offered me the sample of tape recorded medical interviews without which plans for this study could not have been realized. In giving me free access to materials collected in their own investigations and through their encouragement of my work, even though our approaches differ, they demonstrated a spirit of true colleagueship.

Extended discussions with Tracy Paget during the development and conduct of the study contributed in many important ways to my understanding both of clinical practice and of problems in research on interviews. I am particularly grateful for her comments at a significant juncture in the work. Her observations stimulated a process of critical reflection that led me to the research strategy of interruption analysis, an approach that is one of the distinctive characteristics of this study.

Several readers of early and later drafts of various chapters took time from their own work to give me detailed comments. I was not always able to make as good use of their criticisms and suggestions as I would have liked, but I know that the book improved with each attempt to respond to their views. For their constructive and responsive readings, I wish to thank Susan Bell, Leon Eisenberg, Richard Frankel, Stuart Hauser, David Reiss, and Howard Waitzkin. I wish also to acknowledge the general encouragement and support of Rita Charon, Cheryl Koopman, Sam Osherson, John Stoeckle, and Joe and Jody Veroff, as well as the comments of participants in my research seminar: Peter Goldenthal, Kyung Kim, Daniel Kindlon, Patricia C. Reinstein, and Thomas Schweitzer.

Finally, it is difficult to specify the many ways, or to mark the limits of the extent to which this work reflects the contributions of Anita L. Mishler, my wife. She has been first and last reader of all that follows. Her views have shaped and clarified my understanding of issues of humaneness in clinical care and research, and of their interdependence. This book is dedicated to her.

This research was funded, in part, by a grant from The Medical Foundation, Inc., for studies of humane medical care, and their support is gratefully acknowledged. I would also like to express my appreciation for the continued encouragement of the Foundation's Research Director, Henry Wechsler; he was sensitive to the fact that a study often takes unexpected turns and encounters unanticipated delays. Salary support that permitted me to devote time to this work came from the Massachusetts Department of Mental Health, the Department of Psychiatry at the Massachusetts Mental Health Center of the Harvard Medical School, and the National Institute of Mental Health through training grants for the Research Training Program in Social and Behavioral Sciences.

The relative ease with which the last step of the study was completed, the preparation of the text for publication, is a tribute to the effort and skill of Linda Christie, who typed the final draft of the manuscript with care, speed, efficiency, and a minimum of error.

CHAPTER 1

Introduction: The Medical Interview and Clinical Practice

Doctor: Wel:l .... what- uh what brought you to the hospital today?

Patient: Well about oh a year- a year and a half ago I se- seemed to be getting a burning sensations (rushinet) right in- probly in here and it wasn't- didn't seem to bad it used to come and go all the time.

Doctor: Hm hm

Patient: And I went to the Soldier's Home they took ..... chest X-rays .... they took cardiogram and uh .... side X-rays but they never seemed to- ... they say that the X-rays don't show nothin .... the cardiogram

                                              [

Doctor: Hm

Patient: didn't show nothin .... but it- for the

                                  [

Doctor: Uh uh

Patient: last year it's getting worse and worse now it seems ta- .... seems to be- .. when I get up in the morning especially .... i- it seems like there's a knife stuck right in throu:gh he:re.

This series of exchanges between a patient and a physician is excerpted from the transcript of a tape recorded medical interview. It is the beginning of the interview and the physician asks a relatively standard opening question: "Wel:l .... what- uh what

1

brought you to the hospital today?'' The patient responds by describing his symptoms, their worsening course, and previously
unsuccessful diagnostic efforts. The physician indicates that he
is attending to the patient's account with occasional nonlexical
responses: "Hm," "Uh uh."

Readers are likely to recognize this talk as a typical opening
sequence in such interviews. However, the notation of the transcript may be unfamiliar. Transcription conventions and rules,
and the reason for this level of detail, will be discussed in later
chapters. As a preliminary guide, a few of the principal features
are noted here: nonlexical utterances, false starts, and repetitions
in speech are retained in the text; lengths of silences are marked
by "..." with each period representing one-tenth of a second;
interruptions and overlaps between speakers are indicated by a
left-hand bracket, "["; speech that remains unclear after repeated
listenings is represented as heard and enclosed in parentheses,
for example, (rushinet).

Later, in the same interview, after a physical examination and
reassurance by the physician about the reasons for additional tests,
the patient surprises him by introducing a new problem.

Doctor: Okay. Why don't you go ahead and put your shirt on here.
...... There are a few things we can do .... to try ....
to evaluate this. Specifically obviously we have in mind
tryin to make sure it's ...... nothing uh .... uh ....
with- involving any of the organs in your abdomen there.
.... Uh:h .... If it is a muscle strain .... then I
would like to say that after we've made sure it's not some
other thing.
[
Patient: Right. Right.
Doctor: I think you'd probably feel better if we kinda .... made
sure it was nothin that (ya wouldn't) need to worry about.
[
Patient: Would that-
Yeah. I wanna ask ya- ud (dknow)- it's nothi- it's- it's
might be a crazy question but (...)
[
Doctor: No go ahead.
Patient: With me more or less wor:rying about that pain and u:h

.... this and that would that u:h .... stop my- ....
well what I me- my sexual .... advancements .... more
or less.

This new problem, sexual difficulties that the patient hypothesizes, and perhaps hopes, are related to his "wor:rying about that pain," is introduced abruptly accompanied by hesitations and other markers of embarrassment: "it's nothi- it's- it's might be a crazy question." The introduction of additional and different problems in this way is not uncommon in medical interviews. Another patient has presented a primary complaint of a "sour stomach." The physician asks when the symptoms occur:

Doctor: And when do you get that?
Patient: .... Wel:l when I eat something wrong.
Doctor: How- How soon after you eat it?
Patient: .... Wel:l ...... Probably an hour .... maybe
less.
[
Doctor: About an hour?
Patient: Maybe less. .... I've cheated and I've been drinking
which I shouldn't have done.
Doctor: .... Does drinking make it worse?
[
Patient: (...)   Ho ho uh ooh Yes.
.... Especially the carbonation and the alcohol.
Doctor: .... Hm hm .... How much do you drink?
Patient: .... I don't know. .. Enough to make me go
to sleep at night .... and that's quite a bit.

In a subtle, yet also embarrassed and hesitant way, the patient has slipped a new problem into the discourse: "I've cheated and I've been drinking which I shouldn't have done." The problem, and the preliminary statement of the condition under which it appears, "Enough to make me go to sleep at night," radically enlarges the domain of relevance for the interview. A few exchanges later, the patient enlarges it still further:

Doctor: How long have you been drinking that heavily?
Patient: .... Since I've been married.

Sometimes it is the patient who is surprised by a physician's line of reasoning and the topic he introduces. For example:

Doctor: Well has it possibly occurred to you, that with all the troubles that yer .... body has gone through, that yer nerves have now got to the point where they suffer, and where you need help to get yer nerves restored.

Patient: .... Uhh ..... Yes. I- I think I'm a bit nervous, ... I- I- I don't see what you mean.
　　　　[

Doctor: 　I-ah I don't-I didn't mean overtly nervous. I meant that
　　　　　　　　　　　　　　　　　　　　　　　　　[
Patient: 　　　　　　　　　　　　　　　　　　No.

Doctor: that ...... yer nerves have suffered to the point that they could be producing some of these pains. .... Becuz I don
　　　　　　　　　　　　　　　　　　　　　　　[
Patient: 　　　　　　　　　　　　　　　　　Ah

Doctor: believe you've got a new tumor evry place you have a new pain. I wouldn't thi:nk of it. No.
　　　　　　　　　[
Patient: 　　　　I'm not lookin for a new tumor, ... no sir, I never said that.

And a bit later:

Patient: I don't- I don't think I have tumors, I'm not .... I'm not lookin for tumors. .... I jus- there's a reason fer my not feelin this: *good* n I don't think it's nerves because I've had .... ahh

Doctor: .... Tch. What do you think it could be?

Patient: .... I have *no* idea. I- I really don't know.

Later the physician comments: "at least y- you have recorded a normal physical exam. I- there's no *no* evidence of illness that I can find in you." Towards the end of the interview, the following exchange takes place:

Doctor: I'm sure that your basic health is good.

Patient: hhh Oh Doctor, I'd kiss you if I were sure you were right.

Medical interviews constitute a significant part of the day-to-day practice of clinical medicine. Some of the typical ways in which patients and physicians talk to each other in these situations are represented in the above excerpts. Patients describe their symptoms and complaints, occasionally surprising physicians by their particular concerns. Physicians ask a variety of detailed questions, evaluate patients' accounts, comment on their general state of health, and suggest reasons for their problem and possible courses of action. Such transcripts, and the tape recorded interviews from which they are derived, are documents that reveal the forms and qualities of clinical work. The study reported in this monograph focuses on the analysis of these documents. The central aim of the research is to arrive at an understanding of how clinical work is done.

This preliminary statement of direction and intention must serve for the moment as a general orientation to the study. The particular meaning and significance of the guiding idea, that the analysis of talk between patients and physicians is a primary source for understanding clinical work, will be developed and specified in the reporting of methods, findings, and interpretations of data.

Several related questions varying in depth and generality will be explored in the study. There is, for example, a first-order or descriptive question as to whether medical interviews have a characteristic or typical structure. Do they exhibit a pattern that is sufficiently strong and consistent to mark them as distinctive social events, meriting and demanding further analysis? The illustrative excerpts with which this chapter began appear recognizable and familiar to anyone who has been either a patient or a physician. They suggest that there is something typical about such interviews, both in form and content. Can useful, systematic, and appropriate methods be developed and applied to the study of interviews that would serve to isolate this structure and determine its essential features? What variations may be found within the basic type?

There are, additionally, a number of second-order or interpretive questions that refer to the significance of this structure for understanding the nature of clinical practice. What function does it serve, that is, how does it shape and organize the medical interview as a particular type of discourse? What type of relationship between patient and physician does it express and affirm? In what ways does the verbal exchange reveal differences in the meanings of problems and their respective understandings? How are these understandings related to differences in general perspectives, on the one hand, of physicians framing questions and making recommendations within the technical-scientific standpoint of the biomedical model, and on the other hand, of patients with orientations grounded in the concerns of daily life? How are such differences resolved?

Finally, a broader question motivates this study, namely, what constitutes a humane practice.[1] This might seem to lie outside the boundary defined by the usual research questions directed to the description, analysis, and interpretation of empirical data. Clearly, the latter are essential questions and will be addressed in detail. Nonetheless, observations of clinical practice are of more than neutral import; they both reflect and bear directly on issues of value. A central and pervasive concern of this study is whether current forms of clinical practice are consistent with and affirm criteria of humane care, that is, respect for the dignity of patients as persons and recognition of their problems within the context of their lifeworlds of meaning. An effort will be made to define these criteria empirically by specifying features of medical interviews that display a responsiveness to patients' attempts to construct meaningful accounts of their problems and, further, encourage the development of non-coercive discourse based on norms of reciprocity rather than of dominance-subordination.[2]

---

[1] The question of what constitutes a humane practice is not added on to the study as an afterthought but has been an integral part of the work since its inception. The grant proposal submitted to The Medical Foundation, Inc. for support of this research was done in response to its request for applications addressed to the problem of humane medical care (see Mishler, 1979b). The Foundation's approval and support of this work indicates recognition of the relevance of studies of medical interviews to issues of humane care.

[2] This preliminary and brief statement of humane care requires elaboration and this is done over the course of the volume. The definition adopted here, although it differs slightly in focus and emphasis, is generally consistent with the criteria for "humanized care" set out by the Subcommittee on the Humanization of Health Care of the Medical Sociology Section of the American Sociological Association. The Committee lists eight conditions as "necessary and sufficient" for humanized care, including a view of patients as autonomous, unique, and irreplaceable "whole persons," who are treated with empathy and warmth, and share in decisions with physicians in a reciprocal and equalitarian relationship (see Howard, Davis, Pope, & Ruzek, 1977).

From this brief statement of questions that will be addressed and the general approach to be followed, it may be evident that this volume is directed both to clinical practitioners and to researchers, particularly social scientists in a variety of disciplines who are engaged in the study of talk. I recognize the difficulty of writing a book that will be equally relevant and of interest to groups that differ widely in background, training, and the goals of their work. Nevertheless, it does seem important to maintain this double intention. The practical implications of research findings cannot be adequately understood, nor effectively implemented, unless there is understanding of the methods that produce the findings. This book, therefore, is both highly attentive to methodological issues and detailed in its report of methods and procedures. At the same time, significant and meaningful research requires more than methodological rigor. It depends on a reflective understanding of clinical practice that does not naively incorporate the perspectives and assumptions of practitioners. Researchers, therefore, must approach the study of clinical work within the framework of a more general theory of society and its institutions. Further, as noted earlier, the study of practice is not neutral so this investigation reflects an explicit concern with and commitment to the criteria of a humane clinical practice.

These considerations suggest the scope and complexity of the work. In weaving together these different strands—observations of clinical practice as well as the methods for studying them, and interpretations of the interactional and discourse functions of interview structures as well as their implications for humane care—the goal is to achieve an empirically-grounded and theoretically meaningful understanding of clinical practice.

To answer the questions posed in ways consistent with and directed towards the objectives stated above, an innovative research strategy is developed. It includes nontraditional methods for the analysis of discourse, a somewhat unorthodox form of reporting findings from successive stages of the study, and a reconceptualization of the features and functions of clinical practice. Using this approach, the grounds for interpretation shift in the course of the work from assumptions based on the biomedical model of physicians to the perspective of patients and the lifeworld contexts of their problems.

The point of departure for this research is to treat medical interviews as a form of discourse, that is, as meaningful talk between patients and physicians. Further, this discourse is viewed seriously; it is not "mere" talk, but the work that doctor and patient do together as an essential and critical component of clinical practice.

This assumption, that the talk between patients and physicians is serious and has clinical significance, informs the intensive investigation of medical interviews reported in the following chapters. However, it merits brief comment in this introduction, since the empirical study of clinical interviews has received little attention in the most prominent traditions of social science research on health care and medical practice. Thus, although problems of physician-patient relationships receive a good deal of discussion, it often takes the form of rhetoric, exhortation, and policy pronouncements rather than of analysis based on direct observation of doctor-patient encounters. Alternatively, characteristics of the relationship may be inferred from studies of the economics of health care or of the social organization of health care delivery systems. Until relatively recently, there were few studies that systematically examined medical interviews as loci of realization of these relationships.[3]

A fairly typical example of the combination of general interest in the topic with a lack of attention to its particulars is found in a recent volume reporting the proceedings of an international conference. It is entitled *The Doctor-Patient Relationship in the Changing Health Scene* (Gallagher, 1978). Gallagher, the conference organizer and editor of the proceedings, begins the volume by asserting that "the relationship between the patient and the doctor is a basic element in health care," and suggests that an aim of the conference is to answer the question, "What is the current state of the doctor-patient relationship" (p. 1). Nonetheless, a review of the more than 20 original papers and of the comments and discussions included in the volume reveals scant attention to the actual interaction between patients and physicians; no interview records are presented or used as the basis for interpretations of the doctor-patient relationship. In his Epilogue to the conference, Parsons recognizes this emphasis: "From the social science point of view it is conspicuous that the main preoccupation of the conference was with what we call macrosocial

---

[3] The work reported in this monograph is one of a growing number of investigations of patient-physician interaction undertaken in recent years. For example, see the papers collected in Fisher and Todd (1983).

problems" (p. 445). He goes on to point out that "...the more intimate aspect of the doctor-patient relationship seems not to have figured very prominently in the conference" (p. 446). Although Parsons does not pursue this point by suggesting studies of clinical practice, it seems evident that an understanding of the more "intimate" aspects of this relationship would require direct investigation of the interaction between patients and physicians.

The conferees represented are leading figures in their fields—researchers, educators, theorists, and policy makers. It is evident from the text that the conduct of patients and physicians, that is, the actual "stuff" of clinical practice, is peripheral to how they frame the central issues of a conference focused on the doctor-patient relationship. Perhaps it is nearer the mark to say that assumptions about clinical practice underlie their analyses and recommendations, but these assumptions are implicit and unexamined.

This emphasis on what Parsons refers to as "macrosocial" problems is not unusual among both investigators and policy makers. It reflects a well-developed approach to the analysis of health-care systems that focuses on economic, structural, and organizational issues. Although this approach need not preclude attention to the features of clinical practice as they are expressed in the interaction between patients and physicians, these topics are notably absent from serious and critical discussions of macrosocial problems in health care.[4] This pattern of relative neglect of clinical practice among commentators on the health scene has its counterpart in medical education and training, although the reason is quite different and reflects the dominance of the biomedical model.[5] The impact of this model on clinical training is profound. Hospitals and emergency rooms are the primary settings within which medical students, interns, and residents see patients and they have little opportunity for work with patients in the context of general medical practice. Training in situations of inpatient care and treatment tends to emphasize technical-scientific skills and the diagnosis of specific diseases; rather than the patient being viewed as a person, the person is viewed as a

---

[4] Some examples of critical analyses of the health care system from a macrosocial perspective that are of considerable significance and value but, at the same time, do not address issues of clinical practice are Ehrenreich and Ehrenreich, (1971), Krause (1977), Navarro (1976), and Waitzkin and Waterman (1974).

[5] For discussion of the assumptions of the biomedical model and its dominance in modern medicine see Mishler (1981).

patient. Diagnosis, care, and treatment are short-term and they focus on single episodes of illness in patients whom students are unlikely to see again. Thus, training differs in significant ways from general practice, where physicians enter into long-term relationships with patients whose life circumstances they become familiar with as they attend to a variety of episodes and illnesses over an extended period of time.

A related problem is that training in the conduct of interviews constitutes a relatively small part of the standard medical school curriculum. Such training tends to follow the apprenticeship model of much professional education; students observe a senior physician conduct an examination and interview and then try it themselves under supervision and guidance. Problems in understanding what the patient means in the interview tend to be defined as technical, that is, the task is defined as conducting an inquiry in order to arrive at a specific diagnosis of a specific disease. From this perspective, laboratory tests and the results of physical examinations take priority over what can be learned from talking with patients. A striking example emerged in a class discussion of issues in medical training. A medical student reporting the reason given by her supervisor for a negative evaluation of her performance on her clinical rotation said, "I was marked down for spending too much time talking with patients."

The downgrading of "talking with patients" is closely linked to the overwhelming dominance in modern medicine of a technical bioscience orientation. A complex set of assumptions about the biological specificity of disease etiology and symptoms and about the primary function of physicians as applied bioscientists, has excluded from serious concern how variations in clinical practice and in the conduct of medical interviews affect the course and outcome of patients' illnesses. Physicians are viewed as collectors and analyzers of technical information elicited from patients. A patient is, ideally, a passive object responding to the stimuli of a physician's queries. Only the physician's judgment of the relevance and significance of information is retained in the patient's record. There are no external checks on possible distortions or misunderstandings, or of different perceptions by patients of what has been said or left unsaid.[6]

---

[6] The problem of medical errors, for example, has only recently begun to receive serious investigation in such investigations as Bosk (1979), Millman (1977), Paget (1978).

In brief, the medical interview is seen as an analogue to an experiment in physiology or biochemistry. Physicians, as applied bioscientists, ascertain the presence or absence of specific signs or symptoms using technical procedures—questions, laboratory tests, physical examinations. It is assumed that there is an "objective" phenomenon to be found. In the instance of a true experiment, this may be the degree of permeability of a cell membrane or the rate of responsiveness of skeletal muscle tissue to stimulation; in the diagnostic interview, it is the presence or absence of a specific disease or abnormality. A particularly instructive example of this "technical" approach is found in the development of a program designed to teach interviewing procedures to medical students. The program uses actors trained to simulate patients with various diseases. Barrows (1968) argues for the usefulness of this method and notes that one of its many advantages is that: "All necessary aspects of disease complications and prognosis can be freely discussed in front of the simulated patients without concern for their reaction to such information" (p. 674).[7] The objectification of patients and the exclusion of their perceptions and understandings could hardly be stated more clearly.

The view adopted throughout the present work is quite different. The illness "discovered" through the interview is constructed, not found. A diagnosis is a way of interpreting and organizing observations. It is no less real because it is critically dependent on what physicians ask and what they hear, and on what patients report and do not report than it would be if it were based on the results of physical examinations and laboratory tests. Since the discovered illness is, in this sense, partly a function of the talk between a patient and a physician, the study of this talk is central to our understanding of both illness and clinical care. For this reason, it merits close and systematic investigation.

Although language is a topic with a long history of investigation and analysis, the systematic study of discourse between speakers is of relatively recent origin. Within this general area of inquiry, analyses of medical interviews as a specific type of discourse represent a small and specialized field of investigation. Given the newness of the work, we would expect to find that studies are based on different models and assumptions about language and use different methodological approaches. These differences and their implications will be explored in the following chapter where

---

[7] I am indebted to Susan Bell for bringing this article to my attention.

a review and critique of past research on medical interviews is presented. At this point, an overview of the main features of the present study and the strategy of research adopted may be useful as a preliminary guide to the work.

As previously noted, the primary focus of this study is on clinical practice and, in particular, on "how" the work of clinical medicine is done. Central to this work is the talk between patients and physicians; the discourse of medical interviews is its main topic and object of investigation. The assumption that this talk is serious, that it is a core component of clinical work, and that it has real consequences for diagnosis and treatment and for the course and outcome of patients' illnesses, is fundamental and has immediate implications. Foremost among these is the necessity for direct observation and recording of medical interviews. Concomitantly, there is a need for methods that allow for detailed analyses of features of the discourse.

The documents with which this chapter began provide a preview of what is to come. They are drawn from audio tape recordings of real interviews; they are not simulations or training exercises. To permit close analysis, various features of spoken discourse are represented in the transcripts. Thus, there are notations for pauses and hesitations. False starts and repetitions are preserved in the text, as are overlaps and interruptions between speakers. It is assumed, for example, that it makes a difference to the ongoing flow of discourse if a physician expresses his attention by such markers as "hm hm" or "Uh uh" either at a terminal junction or within a clause in a patient's utterance. Discussion of the problem of transcription, and details of transcription and analysis procedures used in this study will be found in the chapters reporting analyses and findings; these brief remarks suggest the general approach that will be taken.

The intimate connection between how a study is done and its findings, between methods and content, is universally recognized; this relationship is not a matter of dispute among scientists or philosophers of science. Nonetheless, this relationship is honored primarily in the form of abstract statements of principle and is rarely acknowledged or explicated in research reports. The most prominent tradition of scientific writing, where methods are presented in a separate section from findings, tends to sever and obscure this connection. Research as praxis, as an extended engagement of an investigator with successive bits of data that are selectively analyzed and manipulated to develop a coherent interpretation, is hidden from view through the use of "standard" measures, experimental procedures, and statistical tests. Not only are subjects and the phenomena of investigation stripped of their contexts, but the process through which the research develops is stripped away in the presentation of findings.[8]

A different research strategy is adopted here. The investigation proceeds through a series of stages. Findings at each stage are then examined critically by reflecting on and questioning the assumptions and methods guiding that stage's line of analysis and interpretation. Essentially, each set of findings is placed in the context of the methods that generate them and the assumptions that underlie their interpretation. A new line of analysis is then developed, based on alternative and sometimes contradictory assumptions. This research strategy will be referred to as "interruption analysis,"[9] since one line of inquiry is interrupted and a new line based on a critique of the first is pursued. The strategy might also be referred to as analysis by critical reflection, as negation analysis, or, more generally, as a dialectical approach. These alternative terms will sometimes be used.

In reporting the results of this work, an effort is made to preserve the process of successive engagements between researcher and data. Thus, rather than concealing this process by recasting results in the form of a standard research report, the methods and findings of each stage are retained and the critical reflections that lead into each successive stage are made explicit.[10] This strategy will become clear as we proceed. The brief and preliminary remarks made here are intended to alert readers to certain significant differences between this report and standard accounts given in studies with which they are likely to be familiar.

In addition to the specific methods of analysis and the research strategy noted above, a model of clinical discourse is developed that allows for the interpretation of findings without having to

---

[8] The notion of context-stripping as a feature of the positivist approach to scientific research is introduced and developed in Mishler (1979a).

[9] The term "interruption analysis" is borrowed from Silverman and Torode (1980). My approach differs from theirs in certain details, but the general thrust and aims of our respective studies are similar.

[10] Since this is an atypical way to report a study, comparable accounts are difficult to find. Two closely-related examples are Carini (1975) and Garfinkel (1976).

rely on the assumptions of the biomedical model. The concept of "voices" is introduced to specify relationships between talk and speakers' underlying frameworks of meaning. Two are distinguished, the "voice of medicine" and the "voice of the lifeworld," representing, respectively, the technical-scientific assumptions of medicine and the natural attitude of everyday life. Differences between these voices and their conflict within the medical interview are examined. These analyses are both the focus and the basis for interpretation of what occurs between patients and physicians in medical interviews. A general line of interpretation is developed through the several stages of analysis that gives primacy to the voice of the lifeworld and to patients' contextual understandings of their problems. In this way, the study moves beyond the assumptions of the biomedical model and its expression in the voice of medicine.

The progressive development of the study and the effort to report it in a way that retains significant features of this movement reflects a view of the interdependence of methods, theory, and values. Studies of social practices, such as the clinical work of physicians with patients, cannot achieve the neutrality that is presumably the hallmark of "pure" or basic scientific research. Without entering into the argument of whether it is achievable in the latter type of inquiry, it is evident that any investigative stance in the study of medical interviews aligns the researcher with one or the other of the competing, and sometimes conflicting, clusters of values, aims, and interests of the participating patients and physicians. Interruption analysis is a mode of reflection that directs attention to the ways that values are embedded in assumptions about methods and theory. In the course of this work, this relationship is demonstrated by showing how the description and analysis of medical interviews, as well as lines of interpretation, reflect an investigator's choice of either the biomedical perspective of physicians or the lifeworld perspective of patients. Thus, the shift over the course of the study at all levels of inquiry—from the form of transcription to the analytic model of the structure of medical interviews and the interpretation of the functions of different types of utterances—involves more than is captured by the term "research strategy." It incorporates a progressive clarification of the meaning of humane clinical care and of the relationship to this value of forms both of clinical practice and research.

In the concluding chapter, relationships between practice and research are addressed directly from the perspective of a commitment to humane values. A definition of humane clinical practice is proposed that includes as essential features the empowerment of patients and the centrality of lifeworld meanings. These features and the values they represent informed and guided the study and emerged more clearly and explicitly as the work progressed. Their explication leads to the development and recommendation of an investigative approach termed critical research.

The methods, strategy of research, and interpretive model used in this study have been designed to achieve its central aim: an understanding of clinical practice. This requires description, analysis, and interpretation of the discourse between patients and physicians since it is through their talk together that clinical work is done. In the next chapter, as context and background to the present study, other research on medical interviews will be reviewed. The form of the review will follow the lines of the overall research strategy described above, that is, I will ''interrupt'' the main directions of research on medical interviews by critically examining methods, assumptions, findings, and interpretations of representative studies. This will serve to highlight through contrast, the special features of the approach used in this study.

CHAPTER 2

Approaches to Research on Medical Interviews: A Critical Review

The central research tradition in the social and behavioral sciences is modeled explicitly on methods that proved successful in the natural and biological sciences. Mainstream research emphasizes the definition and measurement of abstract variables presumed to be highly general, if not universal; the experiment as the ideal research paradigm; and quantification to permit statistical testing of hypotheses. This approach, though still dominant, has been the target of diverse and sustained criticism in recent years. Critics have argued that these "borrowed" methods are inapplicable to the study of significant aspects of human experience and action, particularly to problems of meaning and language. Alternatives to mainstream methods have been developed that are viewed as more appropriate for research on these problems.[1]

On the whole, research on medical interviews reflects the mainstream tradition, however several recent studies adopt an alternative approach. Both types of studies will be reviewed in this chapter. A close examination is undertaken of the assumptions, limitations, and problems of various methods to provide a context within which the main features of the present study will be introduced. As will become evident, my approach relies upon

---

[1] For a critical analysis of mainstream research methods in social and behavioral sciences and of the positivist model on which they are based, see Mishler (1979a) and the references cited therein. This paper proposes several alternative approaches to the study of discourse deriving from sociolinguistics, phenomenology, and ethnomethodology. The argument developed sets the problem for research to which the present study is directed.

the recent critique of mainstream research and the concomitant development of alternative methods.

This review is selective in several respects. First, attention is restricted to studies of the actual talk between patients and physicians. Typically, medical interviews are either observed or tape recorded; analyses of various features of speech then serve as the basis of interpretation. Many studies of the health care system and of patient-physician relationships are excluded by this restriction. Among the exclusions are ethnographic and institutional studies that use fragments or excerpts from interviews or conversations illustratively rather than as data for methodical analysis,[2] as well as studies that rely on retrospective accounts of interviews from patients and/or physicians.[3]

Second, no exhaustive "review of the literature" is attempted. A few well-known and significant studies are examined in some detail and compared with each other. They were selected as representing the main types of approach in this area of research. This further restriction of scope permits analysis of key methodological and theoretical issues within a framework specifying three distinct, though interdependent stages of research: description, analysis, and interpretation. Methodological decisions made at each of these stages are examined to clarify the assumptions of mainstream and alternative approaches and to assess the implications of these decisions for understanding and interpreting findings.

Third, this review focuses primarily on weaknesses and limitations and positive contributions of each of the several studies receive little comment. The intent of this relatively one-sided approach is neither to deny the value of or dismiss the seriousness of other investigators' efforts. They have kept alive an area of inquiry and current recognition and understanding of the many important issues in medical interviews reflects their work. Further, the methodological and theoretical problems that will be discussed are not peculiar to investigations of medical interviews, but are

---

[2] For examples of studies that use excerpts from clinical and research interviews illustratively to describe physician-patient relationships see Emerson (1970) and Duff and Hollingshead (1968).

[3] Studies by Lazare and his coworkers of both the "customer approach" and "negotiation" in psychiatric outpatient clinics, for example, use responses of patients to research interviews to characterize the clinical interview itself (see Lazare & Eisenthal, 1977; Lazare, Eisenthal, & Wasserman, 1975; Lazare, Eisenthal, Wasserman, & Harford, 1975).

generic to research in the social and behavioral sciences. Nonetheless, the development of stronger and more appropriate concepts and methods depends on as rigorous and detailed an analysis as possible of the inadequacies of past research. In a sense, the critical approach adopted here applies the previously described strategy of "interruption analysis" used throughout this work.[4] The initial objective of this critique is to uncover and display the underlying assumptions of the most prominent lines of theorizing and investigation. The second and more important objective is to design a new approach, shaped by the results of this analysis, that is more adequate and appropriate to the problems of studying the discourse of clinical practice.

It is evident from these preliminary remarks that this "review" of medical interview research is narrowly restricted in both scope and intent. It is neither a general introduction nor a survey of principal themes and findings. Rather, it is focused on the interplay of methods, concepts, and theoretical biases and should be read as an integral part of my own inquiry, that is, as one phase of the research reported in this monograph. The encounter with problems for which there were alternative solutions, for example, how to choose among different forms of transcription to represent discourse or how to interpret the functions of the pervasive question-response-question structure found in medical interviews, led me to look closely at the assumptions and consequences of such methodological decisions.

Concern with these issues, viewed from the perspective of an investigator who must make choices at a number of key turning points, has determined the organization, aims, and evaluative perspective of this review. Since a researcher must deal successively in a study with the analytically distinct, though interwoven, problems of description, analysis, and interpretation, the questions

---

[4] It is worth noting that the direction taken in the present study did not originate in a critique of the investigations of others, but emerged from a process of reflective self-criticism; from "interrupting" my own approach to research. The assumptions and methods of description, analysis, and interpretation that characterize mainstream research and are targets of critical analysis in this chapter are represented clearly and prominently in my earlier studies on other topics, and extended reference does not seem appropriate or relevant in the context of this chapter. Nonetheless, the arguments presented here about the problems of standard code-category systems to describe the meaning of speech in context or of the statistical analysis of aggregated frequencies of linguistic features, for example, apply with equal force to my own work (Mishler 1975a, 1978; Mishler & Waxler 1968).

that arise at each of these stages are discussed in that order. A consequence of this approach is that different aspects of the same studies are discussed at different points where decisions about and solutions to problems at each stage are compared.

The aim of this review is also shaped by investigative concerns. I believe that standard solutions to significant research problems in the study of clinical discourse are based on questionable assumptions and, in addition, that there has been little recognition of the implications of these decisions for how the language of medical interviews is interpreted or how clinical practice is understood. A principal task to which this analysis of methodological problems is directed is to make certain issues problematic, that is, to raise questions about underlying taken-for-granted assumptions so that research decisions can be made more reflectively and on more adequate grounds. One result of this intention is that relatively-neglected problems are made prominent and receive detailed explication, for example, serious attention is given to the distinction between speech and written text and to transcribing rules used in different studies.

It will also become clear that this is not a neutral review. That is, I consider certain approaches and methods to be better than others in the strict sense of being more appropriate for the study of meaning and language and more relevant to the task of understanding the nature of humane clinical practice. This directly expresses my view that methods, concepts, and values are interdependent. If methods are not neutral, neither can comparison and assessment of different methods be neutral. Thus, different formulations of the problems of research on language as well as definitions of the goals of patients and physicians in medical interviews both reflect and bear on evaluative positions with regard to the central question of humane clinical practice. Code-category systems, for example, specify what is to be counted as significant and meaningful in patient-physician exchanges and these judgments incorporate theoretical and social biases. An adequate understanding of a study's findings, therefore, requires examination of code-category definitions and the rules for their application. The methodological stance expressed here, through a strong critique of mainstream methods and a recommendation for the use of alternatives that are more respectful of the structure and meaning of spoken discourse, is intimately related to the definition of and perspective on humane clinical care developed in this study.

It was noted earlier that the dominance of mainstream research methods has been challenged in recent years. The critical perspective presented and described here is part of widespread and diverse discontent with the current state of the social and behavioral sciences. Many investigators have shifted away from rigid adherence to traditional recipes for "scientific" research. There is considerable interest, for example, in methods of qualitative field research such as participant observation, ethnography, and in-depth interviewing. Several of the studies of medical interviews discussed below use methods that contrast explicitly with those in the mainstream tradition and draw upon alternative approaches developed in sociolinguistics, ethnomethodology, and conversation analysis. Since these tend to be more recent studies, this may signify that a general shift in orientation is already in progress. Although it is too early to assess the strength of this new movement, it is clear that my own work is only one of a number of efforts to redirect theory and research in the study of clinical discourse.

Description: The Transformation of Observations into Data

Differences between speech and written text are so obvious and striking that it may seem at first a pedantic exercise to detail them and emphasize their significance for research on discourse. Clearly, a range of phenomena that are integral to naturally-occurring speech have no analogue on the printed page, at least in its standard familiar form. Thus, features of speech such as intonation, pitch, pacing, volume, filled and unfilled pauses, nonlexical vocalizations, false starts, repetitions, interruptions, and overlaps between speakers are omitted from the great variety of printed texts even when they include quotations. These omissions are particularly noticeable when the text is presumed to represent speech, as in transcripts of journalistic or research interviews, of courtroom testimony, or of committee hearings.

Despite their usual neglect, it might be expected that in studies of medical interviews these features would receive serious attention and would be preserved in data used for analysis. Their communicative significance to speakers is self-evident. One example may suffice here to make the general point that the meaning of what speakers are saying to each other may be lost, altered, or distorted if the text does not represent certain aspects of the ways in which they are talking. In Chapter 1, a physician's statement to a patient was transcribed to retain his false start and repetition and stress on a word: "I- there's no *no* evidence of illness that I can find in you." In many studies of medical interviews, particularly, as we shall see, those following the mainstream tradition of research, these features would be omitted and the utterance transcribed as follows: "There's no evidence of illness that I can find in you." Our sense of what the physician "meant" is influenced markedly by the differences between these two "transcriptions," and these differences, in turn, have significant consequences for data analysis and the interpretation of findings as well as for our general understanding of clinical work and patient-physician relationships.

Although coding of speech may be done on line, that is, codes or scores can be assigned by observers to ongoing speech without the intermediate step of a prepared typescript, this has not been the procedure usually followed in studies of medical interviews in which investigators have generally applied analytic codes to transcripts. In this step, where raw observations are transformed into texts, investigators are providing a description of their phenomenon of interest. This description, not the speech itself, becomes the object of analysis; it is the data from which findings are generated and on which interpretations are based.

In other areas of research, the gap between observations and data is well-recognized and methods for transforming the former into the latter have been developed in systematic ways. For example, a sophisticated, technical literature exists on the problems and procedures for converting questionnaire-, interview-, and test-responses into scales or factor scores. This has not been the case for mainstream research on medical interviews. In general, the problem has gone unrecognized, and information on the rules and procedures for transcribing speech is not reported. At the least, this makes it difficult to assess reported findings; hence, valid comparisons between studies or replications are neither feasible nor meaningful. As we shall see below, problems of transcription are dealt with more directly by researchers using alternative approaches to the study of discourse.

The preceding generalizations come from a close examination of past research. It is instructive to begin a more detailed review of this work with a study by Korsch and her colleagues, reported in a series of papers (Francis, Korsch, & Morris, 1969; Freemon, Negrete, Davis, & Korsch, 1971; Korsch, Gozzi, & Francis, 1968; Korsch & Negrete, 1972). This is one of the earliest reported studies of medical interviews. It is also particularly germane to the aims of this review since it incorporates a relatively whole-hearted and nonreflective acceptance of mainstream research methods. Examination of this study will allow a clear demonstration of the characteristics of this approach and of its problems. Other studies, some bearing a family resemblance and others using different approaches, will then be discussed and compared.

In the opening paragraph of their first paper, Korsch and her colleagues orient readers to the topic and goal of their research:

> The 'art of medicine' has been the topic of much discussion but has never been subjected to scientific scrutiny. Whereas other aspects of medical practice are included in the physician's training, the approach to the patient is expected to be on the basis of intuition, and it is traditionally learned only by precept and by experience. (1968, p. 855)

They then note widespread problems in patient-physician relationships: "discontent of the community," criticism of the "lack of warmth and humanity in the available medical care," and the "failure of patients to accept medical advice." All of these problems constitute

> further documentation of the breakdown of doctor-patient communication. The present study represents one effort to introduce more objective scientific principles into this important facet of medical practice. (p. 855)

The degree of patient satisfaction or dissatisfaction with medical care and sources of variation in this dimension are a principal interest for Korsch et al. They summarize the types of "communication barriers" found that contribute significantly to patient dissatisfaction:

> notably lack of warmth and friendliness on the part of the doctor, failure to take into account the patient's concerns and expectations from the medical visit, lack of clear-cut explanation concerning diagnosis and causation of illness, and use of medical jargon. (p. 869)

Later studies echo these early findings, particularly when the investigative stance is similar to that of the Korsch group. Reports of "communication barriers," of "gaps," "distortions," and "misunderstandings" recur again and again.[5] For various reasons, based on methodological problems and implicit assumptions about medical care that will be discussed below, these findings, though "replicated," are neither convincing nor definitive; many significant issues about clinical work are unresolved. The essential task of the reanalysis undertaken here is to develop an alternative approach that will provide a deeper and more adequate understanding of medical interviews and clinical practice. In this approach, these findings are treated as problematic: What do they mean and how do they help us understand clinical practice? Answering these questions requires careful and critical examination of relationships between the findings and the methods that produced them. It further requires clarification of the assumptions—methodological, theoretical, ideological—through which investigators interpret and "make sense" of their findings.

Korsch and her associates stress the "scientific" nature of their work. This rhetoric of "scientific method" is a familiar one in mainstream studies. Equally familiar is the emphasis on quantification that appears to be one of their principal criteria for applying "objective scientific principles" to the "art of medicine." The study is based on a relatively large sample: 285 medical interviews were tape recorded, out of a larger sample included in the overall study of 800 patient visits to the Emergency Clinic of a children's hospital, a unit serving generally as a walk-in clinic for many common pediatric problems. The general aim of the research is to explore relationships between specific features of doctor-patient interaction and patient satisfaction and compliance with medical recommendations. Their papers include tables of the distributions of frequencies and percentages of different types of interaction by patients and physicians as defined by the categories of their interaction-coding system, and occasional statistical tests of relationships among variables.

This summary of their general approach, indicating their concern with and attention to rigorous methods, underscores a significant omission in their work. Namely, they do not report how

---

[5] For a review of a number of these studies and discussion of the possible source of this consistent pattern of physician behavior in features of medical education and hospital social organization see Hauser (1981).

the tape recorded interviews were converted into texts for coding and analysis. The only reference to this process occurs in a paragraph on coding procedures in one of the papers: "... a team of two persons audited the tape recordings but coded each interaction on transcribed copies independently" (Korsch et al., 1968, p. 300).[6]

They do not specify their transcription procedures and rules, nor do they present any examples of transcripts (with the exception of one excerpt in a later article in the *Scientific American*, discussed below). Because of these omissions, we lack an adequate description of their object of study, that is, the interaction between patients and physicians. Earlier, I pointed to the obvious differences between speech and text and to the importance of specifying how raw observations, in this case tape recorded interviews, are transformed into data for analysis (transcripts). Without knowledge of this process we cannot properly and systematically assess the meaning or validity of reported findings. This conclusion applies to Korsch et al.'s study since they do not provide information on how speech was transformed into text, even though these texts are the core data for coding, and their analyses and findings refer to the communication patterns indexed by these codes.

A brief transcript of an interview is included in an article written for a more general audience (Korsch & Negrete, 1972), but it serves more to highlight the problem than to clarify it. Utterances by a physician and a patient's mother are arrayed in separate parallel columns. However, it is unclear whether this is the form of the original transcripts or whether it is intended as a more interesting graphic display consistent with other illustrations in the journal. From this transcript, it appears that certain nonlexical expressions such as "Oh" and "Hm" were retained in the texts. On the other hand, the mother's utterances show a level of grammatical precision and unhesitant fluency that is rare in speech. For example, she asks such questions as: "Is that very dangerous when you have a hole in your heart?" and "What was it that caused the hole in his heart?" Further, the transcript shows no

---

[6] The coding procedures used by Korsch et al. were patterned on an earlier study by Davis (1968) who served as a consultant to them and was a coauthor of one of their papers. In a footnote, Davis provides further detail on how coding was done but again only passing reference is made to the transcripts, for example, indicating that unitizing was done on them.

interruptions or overlaps in speech between mother and physician. If, as seems likely, this "transcript" is a normalized version of actual speech, it cannot stand as an adequate description of the interaction and we are no closer to understanding how the work of transcription was done.

It has not been my intention to single out this particular study for harsh criticism. Rather my critique is directed more generally at an approach typified by Korsch et al.'s work. The failure to recognize the gap between speech and text and to deal directly with the problems of transcription is typical of other studies that I have labeled in the mainstream research tradition.

We find a similar neglect of transcription in a large-scale investigation carried out by two British investigators. In their monograph, Byrne and Long (1976) report analyses based on more than 1800 medical consultations, the largest sample base of any study on this topic. Essentially, their book is an instruction manual for the use of an elaborate coding scheme. Each coding category is explicitly defined and illustrated with interview excerpts, case examples show how the full scheme is applied, and suggestions are made for using the system in physician training programs.

There is hardly a page in this monograph that does not include an excerpted exchange between a physician and a patient, and texts of many complete interviews are presented. Despite all this attention to detail and the authors' expressed hope that their work will be used as a model for further research and as a training manual for medical interviewing, there is not a single statement in the book that describes how the tape recorded interviews are transformed into the texts to which the codes are applied.

A few examples, culled at random, show the form of their transcripts.

D "Well, Mrs. T——."
P "I don't know really where to start to tell you. I have pains in my stomach, that's nothing very much. But on Monday I would have tried to commit suicide if I could have managed it."
D "Why was that? Why did you feel so bad?"
P "I am sorry." (Crying)
D "That's quite all right." (p. 97)

D "Good morning. Sit down. Now then. ...."

P "I don't know where to begin."

D "Mmm. Mmm."

P "Well, I'm not really ill and I feel a bit of a fraud."

D "A fraud?"

P "Well, you are supposed to make me better when I'm ill and I'm not ill." (p. 101)

D "What's the trouble?"

P "Well I've been attending Dr S—— for my nerves, I've just recently separated and my home has been sold at B—— and also I've just had a breast growth removed, which has caused me some anxiety."

D "Did they just take the lump? Or the whole breast?"

P "No, just the lump."

D "Who did that?"

P "It was at the Northern, Dr. B——."

D "Have you had the report?"

P "Yes, it was fibroid."

D "That's okay then. Is he seeing you again?" (p. 115)

Clearly, these patients are not presenting trivial problems. It seems highly probable that their accounts are heavily weighted with expressions of distress. However, except for the parenthetical notation (Crying) in the first excerpt, these texts provide no evidence of how patients express their experiences of disturbing events and states of mind shown by statements such as "I would have tried to commit suicide," "I feel a bit of a fraud," and "I've just had a breast growth removed, which has caused me some anxiety." Nor, do we have any indication of what the physicians are expressing in their responses.

Both physicians and patients appear to speak in complete, grammatically correct sentences, and the text shows none of the signs that we would expect to be present if speakers are upset or distressed: false starts, hesitations, nonlexical expressions, overlaps and interruptions. Because of these omissions, we cannot accurately "read" the meanings conveyed in these stretches of talk. Rather, we "read" them intuitively, with full recognition of the fact that they are not "true" records of speech. We interpret by interpolation, that is, we insert the missing expressive signs and thereby manage to make sense of what is being said. But, in doing this unreflectively and implicitly, we are no longer basing our interpretations on the discourse itself. Instead, we are relying on our own competence as native speakers, listeners, and readers for our understanding. This competence allows us to read "between the lines," to interpolate-interpret so naturally and easily that we are usually unaware that the "signs" requisite for interpretation are missing from the text, unless it is brought to our attention through an analysis such as the present one. Some of the implications of these problems for coding and analysis will be discussed in the following section.

A third study, similar in general approach and methods to those discussed above, will serve as a final example. Waitzkin, Stoeckle, and their colleagues (1972, 1976; Waitzkin, Stoeckle, Beller, & Mons, 1978) collected a large sample of 481 tape recorded doctor-patient encounters, including physicians in private practice as well as in outpatient clinics.[7] Their study focuses on the "informative process in medical care," which they define specifically as the "communication of information about illness" in the medical interview. Unfortunately, the criticisms of the Korsch et al. and Byrne and Long studies apply here as well; issues of transcription receive no attention. This neglect is particularly noticeable in this study since it employs a more sophisticated methodology than the others: systematic attention is directed to problems of research design, the classification of types of variables within a general conceptual framework, the empirical evaluation of coding systems, and the design of statistical analyses for testing hypotheses. Although they are attentive to many other methodological issues, Waitzkin and Stoeckle remark only in passing about the critical step of transcription. In the course of discussing measurement of their main dependent variable, that is, a physician's communication of information about illness they say: "To measure this variable, doctor-patient interaction is directly recorded and analyzed. ... Transcripts are prepared of those parts of the recorded interaction in which information is requested by patients and/or conveyed by doctors" (Waitzkin et al., 1978, p. 319).

---

[7] Waitzkin and Stoeckle's sample is the source for the series of medical interviews used in my work and reported in this volume. I have already acknowledged their generosity in sharing their materials with me. I also served as an occasional consultant to their project. My connection with their work underscores and reinforces the point made above that the critical thrust of the present chapter is directed at an approach to research represented not only in the work of other investigators examined here, but in my own earlier studies.

Taken together, the studies by Korsch et al., Byrne and Long, and Waitzkin et al. comprise a significantly large proportion of the research on medical interviews that focuses directly on features of interaction between physicians and patients. This alone would warrant our giving them detailed and critical attention. They have been grouped together for the purpose of this review since they represent an application of the mainstream tradition of research in the social and behavioral sciences to this area of inquiry.

In recent years, a number of investigators have used alternative approaches to study clinical interviews. Of particular interest are studies that draw upon the methods and research perspectives of sociolinguistics, ethnomethodology, and phenomenology.[8] Although there is variation among these approaches, they each share an orientation to speech as a serious topic for research. In this respect, as well as in their attention to transcription methods, they contrast markedly with the studies that represent the mainstream research tradition.

The application of a sociolinguistic approach to the study of clinical interviews is well represented in the recent monograph by Labov and Fanshel (1977). Their entire book is taken up with a detailed analysis of one 15-minute segment taken from a session between a patient and her psychotherapist. This degree of attention to a single interview is in sharp and striking contrast to the large samples included in the studies reviewed earlier. In large part, this difference reflects the intense concentration of Labov and Fanshel on the qualities of speech and the interactional functions of different features of speech such as intonation, hesitancies and breaks in fluency, and other paralinguistic features.

Labov and Fanshel are primarily interested in the interactional functions of speech, that is, in what is being "done" by speakers through their ways of talking. Thus they develop an elaborate set of codes for different types of requests and responses to requests, and allow for multiple levels of meanings; some requests may be challenges by the other speaker and some responses may be indirect. They classify many nonsemantic and nonsyntactic features as "cues" and view them as carriers of affect that can modify the meaning of words. They also introduce a number of graphic devices for displaying the various features and functions of speech.

---

[8] These three alternative approaches are contrasted with mainstream research methods and proposed as more appropriate to studies of discourse in Mishler (1979b).

We would expect their transcripts to be quite different from those shown earlier. These differences are evident in the following excerpt:

1.1[a] R: I don't .. know, whether ... I- I think I did- the right thing, jistalittle .. situation came up .... an' I tried to uhm ...... well, try to ....use what I- what I've learned here, see if it worked.

   [b] Th: Mhm.

   [c] R: Now, I don't know if I did the right thing.

1.2[a] R: Sunday .. um- my mother went to my sister's again.

   [b] Th: Mm-hm.

   [c] R: And she usu'lly goes f-r about a day or so, like if she leaves on Sunday, she'll come back Tuesday morning. [Hm] So- it's nothing

1.3[a] R: But- she lef' Sunday, and she's still not home.

   [b] Th: O-oh.

   [c] R: And .. I'm gettin' a little nuts a'ready. (p. 363)

Certain qualities of naturally-occurring speech are represented in this transcript that are omitted in transcripts reported by researchers following the mainstream tradition. For example, words and phrases that were apparently spoken in a nonstandard way are spelled in the text as they are heard: "jistalittle," "lef'," "a' ready." Pauses within a speaker's utterance are noted by dots, "...", each dot representing 0.5 seconds. At a more complex level which reflects Labov and Fanshel's interpretation of meanings in the text, they divide the interview into a series of episodes, each organized around a major theme or topic; within each episode there are shorter exchange sequences that focus on a subtopic. These groupings are indicated at the left of the transcript by numbers and letters; thus, "1.1" is the first exchange in the first episode, "1.2" the second exchange in this episode, and so forth. The partitioning of utterances into sub-episodes highlights an important and unusual aspect of Labov and Fanshel's conceptualization of the meanings and functions of speech, namely, that a speaker's single utterance may have a plurality of topical references and should therefore be divided into different episodes or sub-episodes. For example, the client's statement: "Now, I don't know if I did the right thing. . . . Sunday .. um- my mother went to my sister's again," has been partitioned by placing the first sentence in "1.1" and the second in "1.2."

Other investigators working within alternative theoretical and research frameworks approach the problems of transcribing speech into text with a degree of attention equal to that of Labov and Fanshel, although their different interests lead to transcripts somewhat different in appearance. Conversation analysts who base their approach in ethnomethodology,[9] have centered their theoretical and empirical studies on the analysis of speech as a set of "social practices" and on conversation as a jointly-constructed and -sustained activity. They have been particularly interested in certain conversational "structures," for example, of the turn-taking system (Sacks, Schegloff, & Jefferson, 1974; Schenkein, 1978) and how conversations are initiated and terminated. Although we would expect some overlap with the texts found in Labov and Fanshel, the transcripts display some differences. The following examples are from Frankel's study of medical interviews.[10]

1. Dr: D'you think y' cam give me a m- *moment* when this happened to yih,
   (1.4)
   Pt: Uh::m, (0.9) Y'mean did I call you when it first happened? =
   Dr: = Mmh hmh
   (0.5)
   Pt: Let's see hhI cal:led, Frid'y (1.0) Uh::m hhh
   Y'mean th' sh*or*tness of br*ea*:th,
   Dr: Ye:p
   (0.8)
   Dr: Hev y'hed any p*a*lpitations? (p. 37)

2. Dr: Did y'feel s*i*ck.
   (0.6)

[9] The first statement of this approach may be found in Garfinkel (1967). Useful secondary sources that are both critical and sympathetic to this development in sociology are Filmer, Phillipson, Silverman, and Walsh (1972) and Wooton (1975). Further developments of Garfinkel's work that are particularly relevant to studies of language and discourse are Garfinkel and Sacks (1970), and Garfinkel (1976). Several examples of recent studies by conversation analysts are Schenkein (1978) and Psathas (1979).

[10] See Frankel (in press). A number of other studies of medical interviews that draw on the perspectives of ethnomethodology and conversation analysis are included in Fisher and Todd (1983); and Frankel (1984).

Pt: A little bit. //Ye:s]
Dr: Mmh hmh.] Right. hh Now c'n yih // tell me-
Pt: An I wz very white
    (0.3)
Dr: Pale?
Pt: Pa:le. (p. 27)

Conversation analysts have attempted to make explicit their rules and procedures for transcription and to standardize the format of their typescripts.[11] From their excerpts, it is clear that they have a special interest in pauses and hesitations in speech, both within and between speaker utterances, and mark them in the fine-grained detail of tenths of seconds. They note variation in stress by underlining and capitalizing syllables and words, the stretching of words by colons ("Pa:le."), and nonlexical features, such as the intake of breath, by "hh.". In accord with their orientation to conversation as a joint product of speakers, they are also especially attentive to interruptions and overlaps between speakers, representing them by slash marks and brackets ("// [").

Our last example of an approach to transcription is drawn from Paget's studies of interviewing and her exploration of various ways of transcribing speech (1981b; 1983a, b). Paget combines a phenomenological interest in levels and structures of meaning with the conversation analyst's detailed attention to features and qualities of speech. She has developed a transcription procedure that attempts to capture the intonation contours and rhythms of speech. Representation of pauses and silences is a critical element in her approach as they punctuate the flow of talk and provide for its organization into units of meaning. In her transcripts, the lines of text display the rhythm of speech in that each line is terminated by a relatively long pause. Further, these breaks or disjunctions in the stream of talk appear to correspond to changes in meaning and/or the introduction of new content or new topics. The following excerpt comes from a physician's response to a question about what he did when he became aware of a significant medical error.

I never I don- I cannot uhh
be too critical n my own mind becuz I uh as I see

---

[11]Many conversation analysts use the rules and system of notation developed by Gail Jefferson (see Shenkein, 1978, pp. xi–xvi).

```
        the multiple chances fer fallacy
n the practice of medicine
n uh = h = h I'm increasingly aware that I perrhaps
    trans- made transgressions myself n I jus cannot
    justify attacking another
guhy
even iff uh I suspect hiss motives
even I can jus tr = y keep my patients away from
    em fer instance (p. 2)
```

The aim of this section has been to make the task of transcription problematic; to make explicit the gap between speech and text, and thereby uncover the issues involved in constructing transcripts of medical interviews that are used as the basis for analyses and interpretations. This has been done by examining how different investigators have approached this methodological task. A detailed review of this problem seemed to be a necessary first step since it was evident that researchers in the mainstream tradition, whose studies represent a large share of the work on medical interviews, have not recognized the problematic nature of transcription. Investigators who have addressed the issues of transcription seriously tend to approach the study of discourse from alternative traditions of inquiry—sociolinguistics, ethnomethodology, and phenomenology.

The point of this review has not been to demonstrate the obvious, that there are different styles of investigation; this would imply a position of neutrality. Rather, I am proposing that an adequate description of the talk between patients and physicians is a necessary and critical stage for systematic study of medical interviews. This requires recognition of and attention to the problem of how speech is transformed into text.

When such recognition is lacking, transcriptions turn out to be poor reflections of speech. Of greater consequence, investigators ignore the distortions and inaccuracies in their transcriptions and treat transcribed talk "as if" it represents actual speech. Each step that follows, from coding through analysis to interpretation, relies on implicit and unexamined assumptions about the meaning of what has been said. Essentially, these assumptions are those of common sense; the culturally-shared understandings of what persons "mean" by what they say. They must be introduced to bridge the empty gap between speech and text, since speech itself and the meaning it carries is not recoverable from these transcripts and must be inferred.

A second implication of our analysis is that there is no uniquely best or most adequate form of transcription. We have seen that even among investigators who approach the problem systematically and reflectively—Labov and Fanshel, Frankel, and Paget— there is variation in the form of transcript produced. This results from the fact that the two modes of expression, speech and text, cannot be made fully equivalent: neither can substitute completely for the other. Each transcription of speech is a rendering, to use Garfinkel's expression (personal communication). Depending upon an investigator's interests and model of discourse, different features and qualities of speech are represented by certain signs and markers; the notational system defines what is relevant and how it is to be presented. The marks on the page, dots for the duration of pauses or brackets to indicate points of interruption and overlap, for example, are not the sounds themselves, but they point to the presence of these sounds. They help us to recover a sense of how the real talk sounded.

It may be helpful to think of the speech-text relationship as analogous to the relation between a musical score and the music itself. Musical notation is an exquisitely detailed system of signs. Variation in pitch and duration of individual notes, the structure of chords and phrases, and the speed and loudness with which passages are to be played are all represented in the score. Nonetheless, the score is not the music, nor is it simply similar to a computer program. Translating the score into music, a task similar to that of interpreting speech from a transcript, requires a competent performer, a mastery of the medium that permits "filling in" gaps in the score in order to "make" music.

There is much room for variation in interpretation, and performers at the same level of competence will "read" a score differently. Further, many significant features of music as heard cannot be represented in a score, a characteristic already noted about transcripts of speech. In music these omitted features include the different sound qualities of families of instruments, such as woodwinds compared to strings, and differences in timbre and resonance among instruments of the same type, such as a gold flute compared to a silver one or a Steinway Grand to a Baldwin piano.

An important implication of the unavoidable nonequivalence

of speech and transcript, however detailed the latter, is that investigators must continue to rely upon and return to the original taperecordings to test and evaluate analyses and interpretations. Transcripts are necessary and useful. The availability of detailed transcripts helped conversation analysts discover the structure of the turn-taking system which was not apparent in listening to the smooth and rapid flow of talk (Sachs, Schegloff, & Jefferson, 1974). In addition, transcriptions allow readers to "see" what is being referred to in analysis. Nonetheless, the ultimate test or criterion of adequacy for an interpretation is the speech itself. For that reason, investigators whose works reflect an awareness of the gap between speech and text move back and forth between transcription and taperecording in order to more securely ground their analyses and interpretations. A critical assessment by others of these studies and their findings requires a similar degree of attention to both speech and text.

The preceding consideration of the problem of transcription has guided the way transcripts are prepared and presented in this report. The aim is to develop forms of notation that represent features of speech and discourse significant and relevant to theorizing about and analyzing the discourse of medical interviews. As is evident, the approach adopted relies on the work of other investigators who have addressed this problem directly.

Coding: The Transformation of Descriptions for Analysis

There is an intimate connection among the several stages of a research project—description, measurement, analysis, and interpretation—and the boundaries between them are blurred rather than sharp. Description shades into and is sometimes completely absorbed by instruments and procedures of measurement, theory is incorporated into hypothesis-testing procedures, and the interpretation of findings both constrains and is constrained by the other stages. Nonetheless, it is useful, for the purposes of this review, to distinguish these stages from each other in order to compare different approaches. The previous section focused on description; here, attention shifts to coding and analysis. I will be primarily concerned with what investigators do with their descriptions of medical interviews, that is, their collections of taperecordings and transcripts.

Coding refers to a methodic procedure for classifying events and behaviors. It is a form of nominal measurement through which specified units or aspects of interaction—observed, recorded, or transcribed—are labeled and sorted into categories. As with all measurement procedures, coding prepares data for further analysis by reducing its volume and arranging it in a standardized form. In the same way that descriptions, such as transcripts, are transformations of observations, coded data are transformations of descriptions.

Coding is integral to many types and areas of research in the social and behavioral sciences; it is used in content analysis of documents, for example, and in survey interviews and observational studies of social interaction. A number of standard coding systems have been developed in the latter area of inquiry and are widely applied. Some researchers have adopted one of the standard schemes for studies of medical interviews; others have designed their own systems, emphasizing specific features of patient-physician interaction that they consider relevant and significant.

Korsch et al.'s study, which served as an instructive example in the preceding section on transcribing, again offers a good point of departure for examining different approaches to coding. Korsch et al. (1968) coded the talk of doctors, mothers, and children in their sample of pediatric interviews using Bales' Interaction Process Analysis (IPA) system (Bales, 1950a, b). Designed originally for the study of interaction in small problem-solving groups, Bales' system has been used extensively since it was first described more than 30 years ago. Weick (1968), in his review of systematic observation methods, refers to IPA as the "best-known category system" and as an instrument with "surprising longevity" (p. 396, 398). Simon and Boyer (1970) make a similar observation, in their anthology of behavior-observation systems: "... perhaps the most widely known and used observation instrument for recording data about interaction in small groups" (pp. 31–32).

The choice by Korsch et al. of the IPA system was clearly not idiosyncratic; at the time they began their work, few other general coding schemes were available. The reasons they offer for using a standardized system designed to code any type of interaction in any type of setting, can stand for the views of other investigators who make the same choice. In the most extended report of their findings from interaction analyses, they state:

> For analysis of the taperecorded interaction Bales' Interaction

Process Analysis was chosen because it allowed for quantification of the interaction into distinctive units designed to capture the nature of the communication process itself. In addition, this method enabled the interaction data to be compared with other variables in this study as well as with other studies. (Freemon et al., 1971, p. 299)

Unfortunately, coding is much more complex than would appear from this deceptively simple and straightforward statement; the promises made are difficult to keep. The critical and unavoidable problem is that human judgment is integral and essential to coding procedures. The coder is the instrument, as might more easily be kept in mind if the method were referred to as a "coder system" rather than a "coding system." A coding manual is a dictionary or lexicon; as is true of all language learning, the meanings of the words are learned and internalized through practice. Some years ago, Fries (1965) found that the most-frequently used words had an average number of 24 meanings listed in the Oxford English Dictionary. The different meanings are specified by their contexts of use. We can hardly expect a more restricted range of meanings for codable units of interaction.

The distinctive features of each coding category, their respective ranges of reference, and the contextual grounds for interpreting stretches of speech as instances of specific categories are all governed by "rules" that usually are not, and often cannot, be made fully explicit. These rules are coding conventions that develop through the practices, the mutual exchanges, and discussions among coders of "what belongs where." Each group of coders working on particular studies develops its own practices and conventions; in a sense, each coding group becomes a distinctive subculture. For this reason, comparisons with other studies turn out to be much more difficult and less frequently done than would be expected from the argument made for the use of standard coding schemes. Recognizing this problem, some investigators now offer a coding "service" rather than a coding manual. For example, a team of trained coders, who have achieved a criterion level of inter coder reliability, will code an investigator's tapes or transcripts of marital interaction.[12] This solves the problem of standardization but, at the same time, removes from in-

---

[12] The coders are "standardized" in the use of the manual described in Weiss (1976). A report of its background and use may be found in Weiss, Hops, and Patterson (1973).

vestigators a full understanding of the interpretive process through which units of interaction are coded, and thereby given meaning.

It is clear from the above that training is a central issue in the development and use of a coding system. Procedures for assessing and determining the adequacy of levels of intercoder agreement, or reliability, are a related and equally important problem. These difficulties are well-recognized. Indeed, Weick (1968) complains that there has been an overemphasis on these issues to the neglect of others: "... observers have spent more time worrying about issues of categorizing and training than about issues of the setting for observation or response measures" (p. 359).

The intent of these remarks on the complexities of coding, and the problems of training and reliability, is to call attention to their neglect by Korsch and her co-investigators. They give passing recognition to the difficulties of applying the IPA system, referring to it as "interpretive," but they do not describe how coders were trained, or how they dealt with such pervasive and persistent problems as the establishment of coding units, conventions for using prior and succeeding acts as contexts, and the rules for interpreting paralinguistic features of speech although they note that "... strong agreement included signs of genuine understanding, agreement, or intention to comply and was coded mostly by the strongly affirmative tone of the voice" (Freemon et al. 1971, pp. 299–300).

Their discussion of the many issues of coding is restricted to the following summary comment:

> Because of the interpretive nature of the codes, a team of two persons audited the tape recording but coded each interaction on transcribed copies independently and then came to mutual agreement on the most suitable codes. Coding reliability was checked periodically and averaged 81% agreement on the modified set of Bales categories and 84% when these were collapsed to the original 12. (Freemon et al., 1971, p. 300)

Eighty to eighty-five percent coding reliability is high in terms of absolute percentages and, for that reason, may convey a sense of being "high enough" for research purposes. However, appearances are deceptive, and these percentages are essentially meaningless. Part of the problem is the poor quality of the transcripts that were documented earlier; this would ensure ambiguity and uncertainty in any coding procedure. In addition, the percentage-of-agreement index used artificially inflates the level of reliability. This index is particularly vulnerable to skewed distributions, and marked skewness was a prominent feature of their data. Thus, half of the doctors' statements to mothers fell into one category, "Gives Information," and nine of the other categories showed frequencies of less than 5%. Mothers' acts were skewed almost as much, with two categories, "Giving" and "Asking" for information, accounting for 55% of them (Freemon et al., 1971, p. 301). Given such skewed distributions, it is necessary to use an index of reliability that takes chance levels of agreement into account.[13]

In a review of their experiences over a number of years, a review that is perceptive and unusual in its candor about difficulties and failures, Yarrow and Waxler (1979) describe their efforts to develop reliable and meaningful codes for children's interaction. They begin by observing that inter-observer agreement in their first study was "severely disappointing." Percent agreement between pairs of independent coders ranged from a low of 9% to a high of 77% for different categories of behavior. They conducted a number of studies, varying their coding procedures in different ways, with the purpose of raising levels of intercoder agreement. They conclude their review on a note of guarded optimism:

> It can be concluded from the experience in the seminaturalistic modeling study that one can attain reasonably good reliability from observations in the form of the free flow of behavior, provided the observer's task is somehow restricted in scope. However, there is still a gap between reliability and high reliability. (p. 42)

Yarrow and Waxler specify a number of problems that set limits to the level of coding reliability that can be achieved. They point particularly to several sources of variation that affect coding reliability, such as differences in the type of behavior observed, in the subjects (for example, whether they are boys or girls), and in characteristics of the coders themselves. Their comments on the negative consequences of "an overemphasis" on coding reliability, despite its necessity for research, are worth detailed quotation:

---

[13] An index of coder reliability that takes into account chance levels of agreement between coders is presented in Cohen (1960); an example of its use with the Bales IPA system is presented in Waxler and Mishler (1966). For recent discussion of different approaches to the measurement of reliability with emphasis on the usefulness of the intraclass correlation see Tinsley and Weiss (1975).

> However, an overemphasis in this direction runs the parallel dangers of neglecting sensitivity to the properties of behavior and allowing observer agreement to become an end in itself. ... Observer agreement is often achieved by coding systems that are modified to serve agreement. Codes are generally defined in context-free, sequence-free terms ... In the service of developing agreements, coders establish conventions for determining the boundaries of each code, and for handling the ambiguous events. Conventions can become too foolproof with everything fitted neatly into a set of categories. ... this forces a literalness on the coder, suppresses ambiguities, and does not allow for different meanings and different connections in the behavior to be preserved. Although a good deal of uncertainty often accompanies coding, even though agreement exists, once coding is accomplished, feelings of uncertainty about possibly miscalled behavior begins to subside. Statistical evidence brings assurance; significant relations are forthcoming, and findings appear. But has the behavior been represented by this procedure as well as it should be? Probably not. (pp. 42–43)

Although these observations by Yarrow and Waxler about enforced literalness, suppression of ambiguities, and the subsiding of uncertainties with the emergence of statistical "findings" apply with particular force to the use of standard coding schemes, as illustrated in Korsch et al.'s study, they are equally relevant to, and based on experiences with, coding systems developed for particular purposes. For many investigators, including those whose work reflects the mainstream tradition of research, the presumed advantages of a standard coding system, such as potential comparability with other studies, are undercut by the irrelevance and inappropriateness of the categories for their problems. The language of description represented in such a code is too abstract and crude to capture the particular qualities of interaction that are of interest.

In proposing guidelines for interactional research, Cairns (1979) suggests a preference for codes that are tailored to particular problems and research aims and implies why this would be the preferred alternative:

> The second guideline concerns the nature of the preparation necessary for successful interactional research, whatever the topic and whatever the species. The key is "Know the phenomenon". In that the formulation of codes, designs, and decisions about timing

depends on the prior intimate knowledge of the nature of the interaction-to-be-explained, most successful investigators spend a great deal of time simply learning about the phenomena before making these decisions. ... The time-consuming and often tedious task cannot be assigned to one's research associates unless they are also assigned the responsibility for formulating the rest of the design. ... The major error is to think of the task of category development and decisions about timing to be independent of the discovery and hypothesis-testing process. In interactional designs, these "methodological decisions" are in fact an integral feature of the research task. (p. 198)

The clear implication is that the more deeply and intimately that a phenomenon is "known" by an investigator, the less likely he/she is to find a standard coding system of value.

The approach taken by Byrne and Long (1976) is consistent with Cairns' guideline. They were aware of Bales' IPA system as the "best-known analysis of interactive behavior," but they decided against using it:

The weakness of Bales' approach, however, is that it does not have enough sensitivity. Early attempts, in this research, to apply this approach to the doctor/patient consultations proved inadequate, if only because much doctor behaviour falls under the broad heading of "questioning." ... the ability to make such distinctions [between open-ended and closed-ended questions] is of particular importance. (p. 30)

Byrne and Long develop a coding system that includes more than 60 separate categories, distinguishing between many different types of questions that doctors ask and responses they make to patients. For purposes of coding, they divide the consultation into diagnostic and prescriptive phases, each serving as a specific context for classifying statements. Further, they assign a score to each statement in terms of the degree to which it is "doctor-centered" or "patient-centered." The basic coding unit is defined as a "unit of sense" in which the observer's "sense of [this] collection of words is quite unitary" (p. 31).

Perhaps the most important assumption that Byrne and Long make, in its implications for their study, is that interaction in a medical consultation is essentially a series of cause-effect exchanges in which doctors are the primary causative agents.

When studying interaction one is normally concerned with issues like cause and effect. In a study of doctors consulting, as will be seen, much of their behavior may well be viewed as "cause" and much of patient behavior as "effect". What is more interesting, however, is the discovery that the patient behavior rarely appears to become causative. ... This cause and effect pattern means that it is possible ... to deal with the largest part of the doctor's behaviour without reference to any patient-caused behaviour. Those parts of a doctor's behaviour which are reactive should then become separate studies. We have not undertaken a study of patient behaviour. (p. 11, 13)

The medical bias expressed in this quotation appears in many guises in other studies, therefore, I will return to it later. Here, some problems in Byrne and Long's approach to coding will be noted. The inadequacies of Byrne and Long's typescripts have already been described and it may suffice simply to underline the point that this seriously impairs the usefulness of their coding scheme, despite their elaboration of categories. Their descriptive data (transcripts of medical consultations) cannot serve as valid representations of the talk between physicians and patients. Application of their codes requires so many assumptions and inference about what was really said and how, that the validity of their findings cannot be assessed.

As stated earlier, Byrne and Long's monograph is essentially a manual of instructions for using their coding system: each of the categories is defined and illustrated with excerpts from consultations, examples are provided of how their coding scheme is applied to a full interview, and there are summary charts showing frequency distributions of statements for different types of physicians. The level of detail is unusual, and makes the book especially valuable for investigators. At the same time, because of the detail, various problems with their approach come through with striking clarity.

One general difficulty with coding systems is that they exclude the possibility of multiple codes. That is, each codable unit of interaction is assigned to one, and only one, category. An important reason for this restriction is that multiple codes markedly increase the difficulties of analysis; statistical methods for evaluating or testing the strength of association among variables, for example, depend on an assumption of independence among measures, and this assumption is violated by multiple codes. Byrne and Long's coding procedure follows this general rule. The problem is that it is often difficult understanding why a particular statement has been coded into one category rather than another. For example, the statement "I think that is very silly of you" is used as an example of the category "Chastising the Patient," but "That was a silly thing to do wasn't it" is an example of "Rhetorical Question." "Challenging the Patient" is illustrated by "What do you mean you have not been taking those pills" while "Refusing Patient Ideas" includes "That sort of approach will get you nowhere at all." A statement such as "I find that very hard to believe" falls into the category called "Doubting."

Byrne and Long do not provide information on the reliability of their coding procedure. We do not know how decisions were made to code a statement into one category rather than another, when both would appear to apply. Presumably, as in all coding operations, coders developed "conventions" that allowed them to do their work. We would expect the results of this process to be those pointed out by Yarrow and Waxler (1979, fn 47); an enforced literalness of code meanings and the suppression of ambiguities and uncertainties. Without knowing more about these conventions or about how coding was actually done, there is no basis for assessing their findings and the validity of their description of medical consultations cannot be evaluated.

Furthermore, the reasons usually given for applying standard coding systems to interaction are undermined and lose their force. That is, the justification of this approach as objective and scientific in allowing for quantification, comparability, and replication does not reflect the realities of coding practices. As it turns out, in view of the uncertainties and ambiguities of coding and the development within particular studies of unexplicated conventions and rules, it is not possible to compare one case with another, or evaluate findings or statistical associations across studies.

Two additional problems require comment in concluding this review of Byrne and Long's approach to coding. First, it is evident from the form of presentation that their findings defy summary and do not lend themselves to further statistical analysis. Essentially, the findings are displayed as charts with totals indicating the frequencies of doctors' statements in different categories. These counts are weighted according to the degree to which a statement is viewed as doctor- or patient-centered, and yield "profiles" of scores for different phases of consultations. Although quite detailed, given the 60-plus categories, the analysis remains at a rather primitive level of description. Comparisons between consultations and interpretations of particular profiles of scores are not grounded in systematic rules or procedures and, for this reason, must be considered casual rather than analytic.

Second, Byrne and Long's approach reflects the almost-universal coding procedure of categorizing units of interaction in isolation from their discourse contexts. For purposes of coding, each "unit of sense," in Byrne and Long's terms, is treated as if it was independent of what precedes and follows it. Of course, this is not actually true in practice and some of their codes require knowing what patients have said in order to understand doctors' responses. Nevertheless, context-free coding is an assumption of Byrne and Long's procedure. In the end, verbal acts in the same category are coded with no regard to where they occurred in a discourse and the sequential organization of meaning is ignored. I shall argue that this general approach is inappropriate for the study of discourse. Alternative approaches deal more directly with the essential features of sequence and context.

Waitzkin, Stoeckle, et al. (1978), the third example of the mainstream research tradition that I selected for particular attention, provides an instructive, though implicit, commentary on the utility of standard coding systems. In their work there is a progressive shift in emphasis away from this approach. The primary focus of their research is the amount and type of information physicians provide to patients. They propose to measure the amount of time spent in providing information relative to other phases of the medical interview and they also develop a code to evaluate the level of "technicality" of such information.

In their first paper, Waitzkin and Stoeckle (1972) review other research and outline their own project; they note some of the limitations of methods that code recorded interaction. They remark that compared to case studies and participant observation, this method "sacrifices some sensitivity to the nuances of interaction" and that "the principal problem which remains centers on reliability of measurements," noting that "none of the studies reviewed here reports estimates of reliability, [but] this problem does not appear insurmountable" (p. 206). Nonetheless, Waitzkin and Stoeckle assert their preference for this method: "Our principal conclusion from this methodologic review is that the most valid analysis of the informative process will emerge from direct observation and quantitative categorization of recorded interaction between physicians and patients" (p. 206).

Their second paper was published a few years later, in 1976, and summarizes work on their project. It presents proposed measures and codes for the information variable but also includes a new approach referred to as a "qualitative analysis of the informative process." The reasons offered for this new approach are worth citing:

> From the pre-test it became clear that the above quantitative measures of the dependent variable would not convey adequately many of the nuances of the interaction between doctors and patients. Therefore, a qualitative analysis of the informative process has been developed, based on transcripts of tape-recorded interaction. (p. 268)

Two qualitative approaches are mentioned. One uses judges to rate typescripts along the dimension of autonomy- vs. power-enhancing communications. The second involves what appears to be an interpretive reading of the typescripts to determine "gaps in communication" or "discrepancies" between patients' understandings of illness and physicians' explanations and an examination of "the process by which physicians translate scientific terms into the everyday language of patients" (p. 268).

By the third and last paper in their series of preliminary "progress" reports (Waitzkin et al., 1978), the emphasis has shifted markedly from their original quantitative analysis of codes to the qualitative analysis of "themes." Almost the entire section on "Preliminary results" is devoted to qualitative analysis; no data is presented from the use of standard codes or from quantitative analyses. The qualitative themes discussed and illustrated with excerpts from the transcripts include: the use of technical synonyms for common-sense concepts, correction of patients' ethnoscientific beliefs, explanations of illness in terms of aging, diminution of implications of symptoms by using less serious diagnostic categories, and the repetition by patients of unanswered questions (Waitzkin et al., 1978).

The shift in emphasis from "quantitative categorization," chosen initially as the "most valid analysis of the informative process," to qualitative analyses that are better able to capture the "nuances" of interaction does not mean that Waitzkin and Stoeckle abandoned their former approach. Their unpublished final Progress Report (Waitzkin, 1978) includes detailed statistical analyses of quantitative measures derived from their codes. Nonetheless, the reasons given for complementing this approach with qualitative analyses are consistent with the questions raised in the present study about the presumed validity and usefulness of standard coding schemes as an approach to the study of interaction.

It will be useful here, as in the earlier section on description and transcription, to contrast the mainstream research tradition of coding to alternative methods for analyzing interaction. In general, alternative approaches apply a theory or model of interaction to the interpretation of discourse rather than a system of standard codes that define units or elements of speech. Put in different terms, their focus is on the grammatical structure or syntax of discourse rather than on its lexicon. Thus, rather than coding manuals, we find formal models of turn-taking (Sacks et al., 1974), or the specification of "rules" for requests and responses to requests (Labov & Fanshel, 1977), or of rules for successful bargaining (Mishler, 1979c). In these studies, attention is directed to the structural organization of sequentially connected utterances. The functional meaning of utterances is interpreted within the framework of the discourse model, or as indicative of the operation of particular rules.

Labov and Fanshel's (1977) study of therapeutic discourse is a particularly instructive example of the differences between these alternative approaches and those discussed earlier. They appear to place a similar emphasis on developing a "code," and yet their use of a coding system represents a quite different methodology. They too refer to the ubiquitous Bales IPA system as "The most carefully articulated paradigm for the study of conversational interaction" (p. 16), but note that, though its reliability is "impressive,"

> the many intuitive steps necessary to perform such a coding have not been explicated. The rich formal texture of conversation is abridged and encapsulated by this device, but there is no possibility of recovering the further structure once such categories are taken as the primitive elements. In this respect, the coding and quantitative classification of conversation is not less intuitive than the theoretical categorizations performed by the psychotherapist. (p. 17)

Labov and Fanshel's criticism of the IPA system suggests the goal to which their own approach will be directed: to make explicit the "intuitive steps" involved in coding and to permit "recovering" the structure of conversation. Although they provide a chart of the primary "speech patterns" with which they will be concerned that, on the surface, resembles a list of codes (p. 61, Figure 5), their "manual" is not a dictionary of terms, but a specification of rules for interpreting the functional meaning of stretches of speech. "Requests" are of central interest and Labov and Fanshel describe a number of types and forms, such as direct and indirect requests and requests for information or action, as well as a variety of negative and positive responses to requests. In contrast to the coding schemes described earlier, Labov and Fanshel do not offer a definition of requests as a category for classifying units of speech, but begin with formally stating a "Rule of Requests" (p. 78). The aim of this rule is to permit investigators to distinguish between "valid" requests and statements that have a request form but serve other functions, such as jokes or insults.

Application of this rule, and of others they describe, in the analysis of discourse requires a high level of contextual understanding on the part of the analyst. For example, the investigator must ascertain whether the hearer believes that the speaker needs the requested action to be performed and has the right to make the request, and further believes that the hearer is both able and obliged to perform the requested act. This is far different from what a coder is expected to understand in order to reliably apply a standard coding system to specific units of interaction.

There are many other innovative features in Labov and Fanshel's analysis, including the detailed presentation of intonation contours, the interpretation of actual speech in terms of its functional or interactional meaning, and the multiple coding of speech acts. All of these represent departures from traditional mainstream methods for the analysis of interaction. The general aim of Labov and Fanshel's research, which holds for other investigators using alternative approaches, is to make explicit how conversationalists themselves make sense of what they are saying to each other. This requires careful and detailed transcription, utilization of paralinguistic features of speech, and the explication of those rules presumably used by conversationalists in deciding, for example, whether a statement is a valid request or a joke, or whether a particular request is also a challenge to one's status in the relationship.

These brief remarks on Labov and Fanshel's work may suffice to indicate the significant ways in which it differs from the studies representing the mainstream tradition of research on interaction. There is great diversity among investigators adopting one or another approach. However, all of them are concerned with the issues focused upon by Labov and Fanshel and all of them attempt to specify the structures and rules of discourse as it is understood and used by speakers. That is, speakers construct meaningful conversations and the investigative task is to describe how speakers do this. The research on medical interviews reported in this book adopts this general aim and develops methods of analysis that are appropriate to it.

Interpretation: The Transformation of Findings into Meaning

To interpret is "To expound the meaning of; to render clear or explicit; to elucidate; to explain" (Oxford University Dictionary, 1955). In the framework adopted here for critical discussion of different approaches to research on medical interviews, interpretation is the third and last phase of a study. Although it is treated as analytically distinct, it is particularly important to bear in mind that there is an intimate connection between interpretation and the methods and procedures of description and analysis. Thus, as we will see below, certain assumptions, both theoretically explicit and normatively implicit, that guide an investigator's interpretation of findings have already been at work in the selection of particular observations as relevant and the form of analysis applied to them.

This discussion will be restricted and is not intended as a full-scale analysis of theoretical frameworks nor of their many and varied sources. Rather, the primary focus of attention will be directed to a general line of interpretation that is evident in much of the research on medical interviews and will be referred to as a medical bias. Along with this bias is a lack of social theory. With respect to the first point, I shall argue that interpretations tend to be based on the presuppositions of physicians about the aims of clinical interviews and the respective interests of patients and physicians. At the same time, the medical interview is treated as if it occurred in a social vacuum. Without a systematic social theory, the medical interview in clinical practice cannot be placed in the broader context of medicine as a social institution and its relation to social issues and society.

We begin our analysis of the problem, once again, with reference to the study by Korsch and her colleagues. Their principal aim was to explain variation in patient satisfaction with medical care and patient compliance with medical advice in terms of differences in features and patterns of doctor-patient interaction. Their analyses used several sociodemographic characteristics of patients as independent variables. The meaning and significance of interaction patterns were interpreted in terms of degree of association with the dependent variables of satisfaction and compliance. Thus, the study used a standard independent-dependent variable research design in which interaction was defined as one of the principal independent variables.

Korsch et al. (1968) offer a number of reasons to justify selecting patient satisfaction as one of their outcome variables. They note that "the wisdom of using patient satisfaction as a yardstick to measure the effectiveness of doctor-patient communication may be questioned, especially since insufficient data are available at this time to demonstrate how and when patient satisfaction correlates with follow-through on medical advice" (p. 866). These reasons include:

> almost universal agreement that one aim on the part of the physician was to meet the patient's needs and to satisfy the patient. ... satisfaction in this investigation correlates completely with reassurance which is another generally accepted goal of communication between pediatricians and patients' parents. ... long-term health behavior and the readiness to consult physicians and clinics for episodes of illness do reflect satisfaction with past medical care received. (p. 866)

The notion of patient compliance is so well-seated in the literature on health care (Blackwell, 1973; Dunbar & Stunkard, 1979; Morrison, 1970; Stimson, 1974) that Korsch et al. saw no need to justify choosing it as the second outcome variable. Because it is generally taken for granted that compliance is a valid measure of medical care, it requires a shift in perspective and some reflection to recognize that the concept incorporates a medical bias. This point may be appreciated when one realizes that although a high proportion of the patients reported that physicians did not fulfill their expectations, physicians were not described as "noncompliant" with patient expectations. The term noncompliance is used in a way that makes it equivalent to deviance, and it is this deviance from the unquestioned norms and values of medicine that provides the basis for interpretation and analysis. Thus, consistent with a research tradition of analyzing deviant cases, Korsch et al. provide "a more intensive scrutiny of the individual patients who had presented noncompliant behavior" (Francis, Korsch, & Morris, 1969, p. 539). No parallel scrutiny of "compliant" patients was undertaken; the assumption behind this asymmetry in their analyses was that compliant equals normal.

Finally, the issue of medical advice is not viewed as problematic. They accept the adequacy, relevance, and validity of a physician's diagnosis and recommendations at face value with no attention to problems of medical error or to variations among physicians. There is no effort to relate compliance to other outcomes, such as the course of an illness or the recovery of patients. In sum, although the variable of compliance refers to the behaviors of *patients* the assumptions are those of medicine in which compliance refers to the degree of conformity to the medical point of view.

Compared to compliance, it might seem that the variable patient satisfaction adopts the patient's point of view. This could be the case in some models of medical care. However, for Korsch et al. it is evident that patient satisfaction is meaningful only to the extent that it is associated with compliance. They examine the relationship between these two variables on "... the general assumption that satisfied patients will be likely to co-operate with the advice they receive" (Francis, Korsch, & Morris, p. 538). No linear relationship is found, but there are differences in compliance between patients at extreme ends of the satisfaction continuum: "... the highly satisfied patients were significantly more compliant than those who were grossly dissatisfied with their clinic visit" (p. 538). They conclude that "a crucial finding is the extent to which compliance is correlated with and perhaps influenced by patient satisfaction." And, rejecting the hypothesis that the direction of causality might be from compliance to satisfaction, they argue that "... the much more probable commonsense explanation seems to be that a patient who is satisfied with the physician would be more apt to carry out the medical advice than one who was unimpressed with the doctor and thought his needs were not met by the medical visit" (p. 539).

The same medical bias is found in the other studies within the mainstream tradition that have been examined here. Byrne and Long (1976) analyzed only physicians' statements in interviews on the assumption that they were "causal" and that patient statements were merely effects. Their description and interpretation of medical consultations is based entirely on what physicians say. Their focus is solely on how doctors conduct their inquiry. They specify phases of the consultation and different physician styles as if these were independent of and unaffected by differences between the behavior of patients during the interview. A similar restriction of attention to physicians' statements is found in Waitzkin et al.'s work (1972, 1976, 1978) in which the major variable examined is the amount and type of information asked for or given by the physician. Waitzkin et al. develop indices of the amount of time spent in this "informative process" and of the level of technicality of physicians' statements, but patients' statements are neglected in both quantitative and qualitative analyses.

The medical bias seems almost inescapable and we even find it in studies that depart from the mainstream research tradition. For example, Labov and Fanshel (1977) cannot be faulted for ignoring what the patient says during the therapeutic session. Patient utterances are examined in detail and a principal aim of their analysis is to understand or interpret the interactional functions or meanings of these statements. However, the medical bias is expressed in a more subtle form in the content of their interpretations. In brief, the meaning of patient statements is provided by the interpretive framework of the therapist; the medical-therapeutic point of view is taken as the grounds for understanding what the patient "really" means. Therapist statements, on the other hand, are accepted at face-value; the therapist, in their analysis, always "really" means what she says. Although the therapist is only one of the two participants in the interview, only her perspective is adopted.

On the whole, the medical bias, although implicit and unreflective, is pervasive in Labov and Fanshel's analyses; the therapist's aim and view of what goes on in therapy are accepted without question. At one point, however, they make explicit their assumption about the proper roles and competences of patients and therapists and suggest how the medical-therapeutic bias has entered into their work. Specifically, they assert that it is in the nature of the therapeutic situation for the therapist to have the "right" to interpret what the patient "really" means and to contest or confirm patient interpretations of her own and others' behaviors.

In elaborating on this assumption, Labov and Fanshel distinguish between "mutually exclusive areas of personal competence," with patients as experts on events in their everyday life and with the therapist as "... an expert at interpreting the emotions of others: The normal claim that an individual might make—'I know what I feel'—is open to question in the therapeutic situation. It would follow that the patient's interpretation of the emotions of others also can be challenged by the therapist" (p. 223). If the patient offers an interpretation, "... the social situation is so defined that she [the therapist] has the right to say to the patient, 'You are not competent to do *this* kind of work [i.e., interpretation of own or others' behavior]' " (p. 223).

Labov and Fanshel's bias, and its implications for their interpretation of therapist-patient interaction, is most fully and clearly expressed in their chapter summarizing the findings of their detailed analyses. The chapter title, "What Has Happened in this Session," is quickly transformed into an attempt to answer the question: "What is the therapist trying to do?" (p. 329). They note that although the patient introduces the topic that serves as the focus for each episode, "... the major initiative for conversation is the therapist's intervention in this area" (pp. 330–1). This recalls Byrne and Long's argument that only the doctors' statements are "causal" in an interview.

Labov and Fanshel select "Masking and Resistance" on the part of patients as a central problem. They propose that patient resistance prolongs and complicates the therapeutic process and is the primary source of difficulties in therapy.

> If the patient could express simply and clearly what she felt and could give a perfectly accurate view of her relations with others, the therapist's problem would be simple. ... The most difficult problem for the therapist is, therefore, to see through the many forms of masking and mitigating behavior that prevent the patient from seeing her own problem clearly and explaining it to others. (pp. 334–5)

In the end, the therapist's task is to see behind the resistance, to discover what is "really" going on, and to communicate her insights effectively to the patient so that the patient accepts these insights as the way to understanding her own behavior.

This is, of course, the therapist's view of her aims, interests, and practices. The crucial point is that Labov and Fanshel accept it as the basis for their interpretation. They do not place the therapeutic viewpoint in a wider context, nor do they critically examine the therapist's statements within the same interpretive framework they apply to the patient. This duality in the interpretation of therapist-patient speech expresses the same medical bias that was found in the other studies reviewed earlier.

Conversation analysis makes a strong claim for the neutrality of the investigator. The goal is to describe speakers' practices and the rules they follow in constructing a conversation; the analyst's presuppositions are to be put aside and speakers are permitted to "speak" for themselves. Nonetheless, the medical bias may slip in through the back door. This may be seen in Frankel's (1981) study of the "organization of gaze, touch, and talk in a medical encounter." In accord with the methodological precepts of his approach, a careful transcription of a pediatric interview was prepared. In addition, Frankel extended the boundaries of conversation analysis by introducing an equally careful description of body movements, gestures, and eye movements; and he developed an analysis that demonstrated orderly relationships among these channels of communication. His intent, as in all studies adopting a similar perspective, was to determine general rules governing the behavior of speakers that result in the apparent orderliness and structure of the interview—an orderliness which he expanded to include relationships among gazing, touching, and talking.

Despite the claim of neutrality, and the restriction of attention to speakers' rules and practices, there is an ambiguity of interpretive stance at the heart of conversation analysis that becomes evident when the work is directed towards understanding interactions that take on special meaning as particular types of social encounter. In a typical study by a conversation analyst, directed to the evaluation of general conversational rules and their formalization, the specific contexts of interaction are stripped away and fragments of talk are examined. Thus, analyses of how turns are taken, or how greeting or questioning is done, are based on collections of isolated instances from a variety of sources. The particulars of content, and of the meanings of exchanges to the participants, are excluded from the analysis. Studies of medical interviews, such as Frankel's, are a form of applied conversation analysis, and have an additional purpose to say something about medical care and clinical practice, as well as about general rules of conversation.

It is this second goal that leads to the problem of interpretive bias since it requires other assumptions and information about "what is going on" than cannot be learned solely from the text of an interview. Silverman and Torode (1980) help to locate the source of this problem by noting that "... the ethnomethodologist must assume that the activity is correctly carried out: he cannot, for example, question the manner in which either [questioning] or [starting] are portrayed or exhibited in this talk" (p. 15). A consequence of this position is that the conversation analyst must accept outside assumptions about the "meaning" of the medical encounter in order to make medically relevant interpretations.

Frankel, for example, in arguing for the relevance of his findings for understanding medical practice, states: "What has been learned? In a practical sense the analysis of this short pediatric transaction appears trivial since neither its content, direction or meaning were problematic to begin with" (1981, p. 23). By treating these issues as nonproblematic, Frankel implicitly accepts the medical definition of the encounter.

The loss of "neutrality" is further evidenced in Frankel's analysis of the physician as the central figure in an interview. For example, his central finding has to do with the effectiveness with which the physician manipulates the patient's attention. Although Frankel suggests that the "manipulation of attention ... is accomplished routinely ... because both parties share similar cultural knowledge about the appropriateness of attending in various interactional settings and situations (p. 23), his own attention is directed primarily to the physician's practices: "One begins to sense a pattern in which the physician is using questions to direct the visual attention of the patient away from the work of the hands and to the task of conversing. ... against this background of appropriateness ... a series of questions ... is being used, strategically, I submit, by the physician in order to maintain a quite particular attentional focus" (p. 21). This is not very different from Byrne and Long's characterization of the physician as the "causative" agent in an interview.

Studies in applied conversation analysis, as exemplified by Frankel, are open to the same criticism that Garfinkel, the founder of ethnomethodology, has directed at mainstream social science research. Garfinkel labels the problem as "Shils' Complaint to Strodtbeck," referring to the latter's proposal to use Bales' IPA system to analyze taperecordings of jury deliberations: "Shils complained: 'By using Bales Interaction Process Analysis I'm sure we'll learn what about a jury's deliberation makes them a small group. But we want to know what about their deliberations makes them a jury' " (Garfinkel, Lynch, & Livingston, 1980). From Frankel's elegant and rigorous analysis of the "organization of gaze, touch, and talk" we may learn much about how a patient and physician conduct a conversation. But, in order to interpret the meaning of this conversation as a medical encounter, the investigator has had to go beyond and behind the conversation. In assuming that neither "content, direction or meaning" are problematic in the medical encounter, he relies on the perspective of the physician to provide the grounds for his interpretation.

The pervasiveness of the medical bias in interpretations of medical interviews makes it difficult to propose an alternative perspective, but it is all the more important to do so. Can the talk of patients and physicians be understood in another way? Can an interpretation be based on the counter assumption that the content, direction, and meaning of the interview are problematic? Paget's (1983a) work is an instructive example of such a possibility, and stands in marked contrast to the other studies reviewed here. Combining a phenomenological approach to the study of meaning with methods drawn from conversation analysis, she adopts what may be viewed as the patient's perspective.

Her account emphasizes misunderstandings between patient and physician, disagreements, ambiguities, and radical shifts in discourse topics. Central to her analysis is "a discovered problem in the talk of this physician and patient," (p. 59) a topic that is not discussed, but of which they are both aware and which intrudes into their discourse: "She is a post-operative cancer patient concerned about the spread of her cancer and about her survival. However, across their three encounters, her condition as a cancer patient and her fear that her cancer would metastasize were never introduced as discourse topics (p. 59). Since this problem was not introduced into the discourse, the patient's concerns could not be addressed.

> Both the referents to her experience of cancer, and the implications of the experience, were lost in the discourse. Instead, her symptoms

were referred to her nerves. She was reassured that her basic health was good. ... Their exchanges became marked by her struggle to resist his diagnostic assessment that the problem was her nerves and by her effort to clarify the meaning of her symptoms. (p. 60)

Medical interviews are instances of "serious talk" that Paget describes as "a labor of understanding, of listening and interpreting, of clarifying and acknowledging what has been said, and responding. It is an interactionally constituted activity sustained by conversationalists" (p. 72). From this perspective, issues of content, direction, and meaning are not settled in advance but are problematic for speakers. In studying medical interviews, the investigator's task is to analyze and interpret how patients and physicians struggle to resolve these issues. Sometimes, as in the interview Paget describes, this effort is not successful and the talk reflects persistent conflict, tension, and misunderstanding.

Conclusion

The principal aim of this review has been to make certain issues problematic for the study of medical interviews. To this end, several approaches have been described in detail and contrasted with each other. The research process has been presented as a series of stages—description, analysis, and interpretation—through which the discourse of patients and physicians is transformed into findings. Methods used at each of these stages have been critically examined to clarify underlying assumptions and to assess the meaning of analyses and findings for understanding clinical practice.

Throughout the review, methods identified with the mainstream tradition of research in the social and behavioral sciences have been compared with the alternative approaches of sociolinguistics, conversation analysis, ethnomethodology, and phenomenological sociology. This analysis has shown that mainstream methods are inappropriate and inadequate for the study of discourse. Essential issues are not recognized as problematic and are, therefore, not addressed; the promise of "objective" and definitive findings is not fulfilled; implicit medical biases distort interpretations of findings. For example, studies designed within this perspective do not take into account the gap between speech and text; transcription is treated casually with no attention to the serious problems involved in transforming observations into data. The transcriptions that result are not adequate representations of speech. For this reason, they cannot bear the weight of the analyses that are applied to them.

Second, those coding systems used as the primary tools of analysis in mainstream studies are faulted in several ways. These systems violate the two most essential features of natural discourse, its organization and structure, and the contextual grounding of meaning. The use of standard coding systems further compounds this problem since the categories in such codes do not refer to the special and particular content of medical interviews. Finally, there is a marked tendency in these studies to interpret findings on the basis of implicit assumptions that reflect a medical bias.

I have argued that investigators working in non-mainstream traditions have developed approaches and methods that address these research issues more adequately and are more appropriate to the study of discourse in medical interviews. They have recognized that the tasks of description, analysis, and interpretation are problematic. Transcriptions are prepared with great care; analytic categories and models of discourse are developed that preserve the organizational and contextual characteristics of speech. Even with these studies, however, interpretations often rely on the medical point of view.

The present study has been shaped by a concern with the issues discussed in this chapter. Clearly, the perspectives and methods of non-mainstream approaches serve as a major resource for this work. The twin objectives of this study are to develop effective and appropriate methods for the study of discourse and, by applying them to the analysis of medical interviews, to extend and deepen our understanding of clinical practice. A strategy of research has been designed to meet these objectives; the results are presented in the following chapters.

CHAPTER 3

Routine Practice: The Voice of Medicine and the Structure of Unremarkable Interviews

Introduction

The work reported here assumes that the discourse of patients with physicians is central to clinical practice and, therefore, warrants systematic study. It will be evident from the detailed analyses that the investigation has been especially shaped by general issues of method and interpretation as discussed in the preceding chapter. Principal features of the approach and the general plan of the study will be outlined briefly in this introductory section.

The inquiry begins with a description and analysis of "unremarkable interviews." This term is applied to stretches of talk between patients and physicians that appear intuitively to be normal and nonproblematic. The interviews are drawn from the large sample collected by Waitzkin and Stoeckle[1] in their study of the

---

[1] Waitzkin and Stoeckle's original corpus of nearly 500 interviews included a stratified random sample of physicians in private and clinic sessions in Boston and Oakland. For the present study, a small series of about 25 tapes was selected initially from the larger sample. Male and female patients were equally represented in the series, and both single and multiple interviews of a patient with the same physician were included. The original tapes were sequentially ordered by code numbers assigned to physicians and each of their successive patients. The selection procedure was to choose the "next" code number in the sequence where the interview met the criteria noted above until the cells were filled. Although this was not a random sampling procedure it ensured heterogeneity among the inter-

informative process in medical care (Waitzkin & Stoeckle, 1976; Waitzkin et al. 1978). In these interviews patients and physicians talk to each other in ways that we, as members of the same culture, recognize as contextually appropriate. Our sense of appropriateness depends on shared and tacit understandings; on commonly held and often implicit assumptions of how to talk and of what to talk about in this situation.

Our intuitive sense of the unremarkable nature of these interviews merely locates the phenomenon for study. The central task of this chapter is to develop and apply concepts and methods that allow us to go through and beyond our ordinary, implicit, and shared understanding of the "normality" and "unremarkableness" of these interviews. The aim is to make explicit features of the talk that produce and warrant our sense as investigators and, by implication, the sense made by physicians and patients that the talk is unremarkable, and that the interview is going as it "should" go. The investigation proceeds through four analytically distinct but intertwined phases discussed in the review of alternative approaches to the study of discourse: description, analysis, interpretation, and interruption.

An adequate description is a prerequisite to further study. As noted earlier, a transcription of speech is neither a neutral or "objective" description. Transcription rules incorporate models of language in that they specify which features of speech are to be recorded and which are to go unremarked. Thus, they define what is relevant and significant. The typescript notation system used here is a modification and simplification of one developed by Gail Jefferson (1978) and used by many conversation analysts; it is included as an Appendix to this chapter. Typescripts have been prepared in accord with these rules. The general aim is to retain details of the talk believed to be significant for clarifying

---

views and there was no reason to believe that the series was biased in a systematic way with reference to the original sample. The analyses presented here are based on a small number of interviews drawn from this series. Further, analyses are restricted to brief excerpts from the full interviews which exemplify issues of primary theoretical interest. This description of the procedure is intended to clarify the grounds on which the claim is made that the interviews examined in this study are "typical" medical interviews. This claim does not rely on statistical criteria or rules for selecting a "representative" sample. Rather, it rests on a shared understanding and recognition of these interviews as "representative," that is, as displays of normatively appropriate talk between patients and physicians.

and understanding the structure and meaning of patient-physician discourse. The relevance of particular details will be demonstrated in the analyses.

In reviewing various approaches to the analysis of discourse, I noted a number of problems in the use of standardized coding systems. A particularly serious limitation is its neglect of the structure and organization of naturally occurring talk between speakers. For this reason alone, this method would be inappropriate to the study of medical interviews which, like other forms of human discourse, is both structured and meaningful. Speaking turns are connected both through the forms of utterances, as in question and answer pairs, and by content. The analyses undertaken here are directed to determining the organization of medical interviews with respect to both form and content.

A structural unit of discourse is proposed that appears to be typical and pervasive in such interviews. It consists of a sequential set of three utterances: Physician Question-Patient Response-Physician Assessment/Next Question. The specific features and functions of this unit will be examined. Problems that arise during the interview are discussed in terms of the disruption and repair of this unit. Finally, the ways in which meaning is developed and organized over the course of the interview are documented and shown to be related to this basic structure.

The effort to make theoretical sense of analytical findings is the work of interpretation, referred to here as the third stage of an investigation. This is usually considered the last stage, but I have adopted a distinction made by Silverman and Torode (1980) between interpretation and interruption. The latter will be discussed below. Interpretations, as would be expected, may take many forms, reflecting different theories of language and of social action. All of them, nonetheless, focus primarily on the questions of "what" is done in and through the talk, and "how" it is done. Thus, in their sociolinguistic analysis of a therapeutic interview, Labov and Fanshel (1977) state their interest as the discovery of "what is being done." They conclude that much of the talk of therapy consists of "requests" and "responses to requests". The framework for the analysis of discourse that they develop and apply is, in large part, a set of definitions, rules, and methods for describing, locating, and interpreting the interactional functions of different types of requests and responses.

The analytic question for ethnomethodologists and conversation analysts shifts towards the "how." For any particular instance of a "request," for example, conversation analysts wish to determine how speakers "do the work" of requesting. That is, how do speakers convey to each other their mutual recognition that what their talk is about is "requesting." But more is involved than a shift from "what" to "how." For conversation analysts, forms of requests and general rules of use cannot be specified and listed in a coding manual, as Labov and Fanshel attempt. The contextual embeddedness of speech would make any such manual a poor guide for conversationalists, and for investigators as well. The "how" of discourse for ethnomethodologists concerns the speaker practices through which "requesting" is routinely done, or "accomplished," to use the ethnomethodologists' term, in any context, despite the problem that a formal rule cannot take into account the specific features of particular contexts.[2]

Much of the work of conversational analysts, like that of sociolinguists, is directed to the study of how general tasks of conversation are accomplished, how conversations are initiated and terminated, how turns are taken, how topics are switched, and how mistakes are repaired. All these conversational tasks are "done" in medical interviews, as in all other types of discourse. One aim of the present study is to determine if there are systematic and typical ways in which patients and physicians accomplish these general tasks of a conversation. For example, there are a number of ways in which speakers may ask and answer questions. How is questioning and answering done by patients and physicians?

Linked to this approach is another level of interpretation that represents a more central topic in our inquiry, namely, the nature of clinical work. Our speakers are physicians and patients, and in how they begin their discourse, take their turns, and take leave of each other they are also doing the work of doctoring and patienting. Interpretation of findings on conversational practices is directed to an understanding of how the work of doctoring and patienting is done. For example, the strong tendency for physicians to ask closed- rather than open-ended questions is interpreted as serving the function of maintaining control over the content of

---

[2] Examples of these studies may be found in Schenkein (1978); and in Psathas (1979). A perceptive discussion of the way that ethnomethodology approaches the study of talk, and some of its unresolved problems, is found in Wooton (1975).

the interview. In turn, this assures the dominance of the biomedical model as the perspective within which patients' statements are interpreted and allows doctors to accomplish the "medical" tasks of diagnosis and prescription. At the same time, the fact that their utterances are almost exclusively in the form of questions gives doctors control of the turn-taking system and, consequently, of the structure and organization of the interview. The interpretation of particular discourse practices developed here will refer to both form and content.

Finally, borrowing from Silverman and Torode, I have referred to a second mode, or line of theorizing, as interruption. Of particular relevance to our purpose is Silverman and Torode's notion of "voices." As I understand it, a voice represents a particular assumption about the relationship between appearance, reality, and language, or, more generally, a "voice" represents a specific normative order. Some discourses are closed and continually re-affirm a single normative order; others are open and include different voices, one of which may interrupt another, thus leading to the possibility of a new "order." There are occasions in medical interviews where the normal and routine practice of clinical work appears to be disrupted. In order to understand both the routine, fluent course of the interview as well as its occasional disruption, a distinction will be introduced between the "voices" representing two different normative orders: the "voice of medicine" and the "voice of the lifeworld." Disruptions of the discourse during interviews appear to mark instances where the "voice of the lifeworld" interrupts the dominant "voice of medicine." How this happens, and whether the discourse is then "opened" or remains "closed" will be of major interest in succeeding analyses.

In sum, the principal aim of this chapter is to develop methods for the study of discourse that are informed by considerations of the research tasks of description, analysis, interpretation, and interruption. The methods are applied to a set of unremarkable interviews to bring out more clearly those features that are associated with our intuitive recognition of the interviews as instances of routine, normal, and ordinary clinical practice. After a close look at how these interviews work to produce a sense of normality and appropriateness, stretches of talk between patients and physicians that depart in some way from the normal and typical pattern will be examined. The departures suggest that something has become problematic. The analysis of problematic interviews is undertaken in the context of the findings from analyses of non-problematic or unremarkable interviews. This will provide an initial set of contrasting features and their functions for use in further analyses that compare the "voice of medicine" with the "voice of the lifeworld."

Unremarkable Medical Interviews

Diagnostic Examination (W:02.014)[3]

The excerpt presented as Transcript 3.1 is taken from the beginning of an interview. Through this opening series of exchanges the patient (P) responds to the physician's (D) questions with a report of her symptoms. After each response, the physician asks for further details or other symptoms with the apparent aim of determining the specific nature of the problem and arriving at a diagnosis. On its surface, their talk proceeds as we would expect in a routine medical interview; it is unremarkable.

The physician initiates the interview with a question that Labov and Fanshel (1977, pp. 88–91) would code as a request for information: "What's the problem." Although its syntactic form is that of an open-ended Wh-question, the physician's voice does not carry question intonation. For that reason, the transcript does not show a question mark. The utterance is a request in the imperative mode, a paraphrase of a statement such as, "Tell me what the problem is." The phrasing of a request for action or information as an imperative is not unusual, and Labov and Fanshel argue that "the imperative is the unmarked form of a request for action" and "the central element in the construction of requests" (pp. 77–78).

In his first turn, the physician has set the general topic of discussion, namely, the patient's "problem." Or, more precisely, the physician's request is mutually understood to be germane and to express their joint recognition of the reason for the patient's presence in this setting: she is there because she has, or believes she has, a medically relevant problem. We, as investigators, knowing that this is a medical interview, are able to "read" the

---

[3] The typescript numbers used here are the codes on the tapes assigned by Waitzkin and Stoeckle; the number is preceded by a "W" to indicate the source.

✓

Transcript 3.1

W:02.014

```
      001 D   What's the problem.
  I ┌                      (Chair noise)
    │                         [
      002 P                        (...) had since . last
      003     Monday evening so it's a week of sore throat
      004 D                                    hm hm
      005 P   which turned into a cold .......... uh:m ........
      006     and then a cough.
      007 D                A cold you mean what? Stuffy nose?
      008 P   uh Stuffy nose yeah not a chest ...... cold. ........
    │                               [
      009 D                        hm hm
      010 P   uhm
    │       [
      011 D   And a cough.
      012 P          And a cough .. which is the most irritating
      013     aspect.  no elaboration asked?, no comments
    └       [
 II ┌ 014 D   Okay. (hh) uh Any fever?
    │ 015 P                   ...... Not that I know of.
      016     .... I took it a couple of times in the beginning
      017     but . haven't felt like-      open ended
    │           [
III ┌ 018 D   hm           How bout your ears?
    │ 019 P                              ........
      020 P   (hh) uhm .... Before anything happened .... I thought
      021     that my ears ...... might have felt a little bit
      022     funny but (....) I haven't got any problem(s).
 IV ┌ 023 D   goes back                        Okay.
IV'│ 024     ........ (hh) Now this uh cough what are you producing
    │ 025     anything or is it a dry cough?
    │ 026 P                        Mostly dry although
    └ 027     ...... a few days . ago it was more mucusy ....
```

IV″ 028   cause there was more (cold). Now (there's) mostly cough.
                   [[

V 029 D   hm hm   What

030   about the nasal discharge? Any?

031 P   ....A little.

032 D   What

033   color is it?

034 P   ...... uh:m .... I don't really know

035   .... uhm I suppose a whitish- (....)
                           [

036 D   hm hm What?

037 P   There's been

038   nothing on the hankerchief.
                [

VI 039 D   hm hm   Okay. .... (hh) Do you have

040   any pressure around your eyes?   *open ended*

041 P   No.

VII 042 D   Okay. How do you feel?

043 P   .... uh:m .... Tired. heh I couldn-(h)

044   I couldn't(h) sleep last night(h) uhm
                           [

045 D   Because of the . cough.
                                 [

046 P   Otherwise-

047   Yup. Otherwise I feel fine.

VIII 048 D   Alright. Now . have you .

049   had good health before (generally).

050 P   Yeah . fine.

                             (1′25″)

physician's utterance in the same way as the patient does. More than simply expressing a mutual understanding of the situation, his request confirms it and by confirming it contributes to the definition of the situation as a medical interview. It is in this sense that the "fact" that a medical interview is taking place is constructed through discourse. Such a definition of the situation excludes others. It is not a social occasion, a casual conversation, or an exchange of gossip, and we do not find initial greetings, an exchange of names, or other courtesies with which such conversations commonly begin. (Their absence must be treated with caution since it may reflect when the taperecorder was turned on).

The patient responds to the physician's request for information; she begins to report her symptoms, when they began, and the change from a sore throat that began a week ago, "which turned into a cold," "and then a cough." As she gives her account, the physician indicates that he is attending to her, understands, and wants her to continue by a go-ahead signal, "hm hm."

As the patient responds to his opening question, the physician requests further clarification and specification: "A cold you mean what? Stuffy nose?" A little later he asks for confirmation of what he heard her say earlier, "And a cough." Through his questions the physician indicates that although he has asked her to talk about the nature of her "problem," the topic remains under his control. That is, his questions define the relevance of particular features in her account. Further, when the patient mentions a cold, sore throat, and cough as her symptoms, the physician suggests additional dimensions and distinctions that may be of medical relevance that the patient has neglected to report. Thus, a "cold" is not a sufficient description for his purpose; he must know what is "meant" by a cold and what kind of cold it is, "Stuffy nose?" The patient recognizes that there are at least two kinds, nose colds and chest colds, and introduces this contrast pair in order to specify her own: "uh stuffy nose yeah not a chest ...... cold."

The physician acknowledges her distinction, "hm hm," and adds to it the other symptom she has mentioned, "And a cough." The patient reconfirms his addition and goes on to give this symptom particular emphasis: "And a cough .. which is the most irritating aspect". The physician's "Okay," inserted to overlap with the end of the patient's utterance, terminates the first cycle of the interview. He acknowledges the adequacy of the patient's response to his opening question, "What's the problem," and his "Okay" serves to close this section of the interview; no more is to be said about the problem in general and he will now proceed with more specific questions.

The first cycle is marked on the transcript by a bracket enclosing utterances 001–014 under Roman Numeral I. Its basic structure may be outlined as consisting of: a request/question from the physician, a response from the patient, and a post-response assessment/acknowledgement by the physician, to which is added a new request/question to begin the next cycle. The remainder of the excerpt is made up of seven additional cycles with structures identical to the first one. The first six cycles focus on the "cold" symptoms, the last two open with more general questions.

There are two variants within the basic structure. In the first type, the basic structure is expanded internally by requests from the physician for clarification or elaboration of the patient's response; this occurs in the first, fifth, and seventh cycles. In the second variant, the physician's assessments are implicit. Although his post-response assessments are usually explicit (an "Okay" or "Alright" comment), there are occasions where they are implicitly conveyed by the physician proceeding immediately to a next question. Alternatively, his assessment may occur before the patient's completion of her utterance through an overlapping "hm hm"; this occurs in the linkage between cycles IV and V.

This three-part utterance sequence is a regular and routine occurrence in the talk between patients and physicians. For that reason, I will refer to it as the basic structural unit of discourse in medical interviews. We recognize and accept interviews with these structures as normal, standard, and appropriate—as unremarkable. The medical interview tends to be constituted, overwhelmingly, by a connected series of such structural units. They are linked together through the physician's post-response assessment utterance that serves the dual function of closing the previous cycle and initiating a new one through his next question.

I do not mean to imply that this structure is unique to medical interviews, although it is one of their distinctive features. The same general type of structure appears in other settings of interaction where the aim is assessment, diagnosis, or selection, that is, when one person has the task of eliciting information from another. Thus, the same three-utterance sequence initiated by questions is found in classroom exchanges between teachers and pupils, although these are not interviews and teachers may direct successive questions to different pupils.[4] We might also expect to find it in psychological test situations and personnel interviews.

---

[4] In earlier studies of classroom interaction, I referred to the set of three utterances initiated by a question as an Interrogative Unit. Connections between units through the dual function of second questions were called Chaining (see Mishler, 1975a, 1975b, 1978).

Further work would be needed to determine how these discourses with similar general structures differed in their particular features.

Since I am proposing that this discourse structure is the basic unit of the medical interview and that its pervasive presence in a linked series is what makes this interview unremarkable, it is important to look more closely at how it is constructed and how it functions. The first and most obvious impression is of the physician's strong and consistent control over the content and development of the interview. Themes of physician dominance and control were referred to earlier in reviewing other studies of medical interviews. However, the methods used in those studies isolated and abstracted physician utterances from the flow of the interview. Byrne and Long (1976), for example, coded only the physicians' statements and summed their weighted scores across an interview to arrive at an overall measure of dominance. Here, I am trying to show how physicians exercise control through the structure of their exchanges with patients in the course of an interview.

There are a number of ways in which the physician uses his position as a speaker in this structure to control the interview: he opens each cycle of discourse with his request/question; he assesses the adequacy of the patient's response; he closes each cycle by using his assessment as a terminating marker; he opens the next cycle by another request/question. Through this pattern of opening and terminating cycles the physician controls the turn-taking process; he decides when the patient should take her turn. He also controls the content of what is to be discussed by selectively attending and responding to certain parts of the patient's statements and by initiating each new topic.

The physician's control of content through the initiation of new topics is particularly evident. After the first cycle in which the patient introduces her problem, there are seven new topics, each introduced by the physician through a question that opens a new cycle. In sequence, the physician asks the patient about: presence of fever, ear problems, type of cough, presence and type of nasal discharge, pressure around her eyes, how she feels, and her general state of health. The list is hardly worth noticing; these are the questions we might expect a physician to ask if a patient reports having a sore throat and a cold. The fit between our expectations and the interview is very close, which is why I have referred to it as an unremarkable interview.

We may learn more, however, about the significance and functions of the physician's control if we examine how his questions not only focus on certain topics, but are selectively inattentive to others. Through the questions he asks the physician constructs and specifies a domain of relevance; in Paolo Freire's phrase, he is "naming the world," the world of relevant matters for him and the patient (Freire, 1968).[5] The topics that the patient introduces, all of which are explicit, but not attended to by the physician, are: the history and course of her symptoms, and the effects they have had on her life—that the cough is the most irritating aspect, that she's tired and has had a sleepless night. Both of these latter topics, opened up by the patient but not pursued by the physician, bear on a question that remains unasked but whose potential "relevance" is close to the surface: why she has come to see the physician at this point even though the problem began a week before.

In summary, this analysis shows that the physician controls the content of the interview, both through his initiation of new topics and through what he attends to and ignores in the patient's reports. Further, there is a systematic bias to his focus of attention; the patient's reports of how the problem developed and how it affects her—the "life contexts" of her symptoms—are systematically ignored. The physician directs his attention solely to physical-medical signs that might be associated with her primary symptoms, such as ear or eye problems, or to the further physical specification of a symptom, such as type of cough or color of nasal discharge.

The discussion to this point illustrates certain features of an approach to discourse analysis that is responsive to the issues raised by the critical review of research on medical interviews in the preceding chapter. First, the "gap" between talk and text has been taken seriously in the preparation of a transcript and the analytic status of the transcript as a "description" of an interview has been evident. The retention in the text of such features of ongoing talk as pauses and interruptions, and certain voice qualities such as question intonation reflects a model of discourse in which these features are assumed to carry functional significance.

---

[5] Another example of the ways in which a physician's selectivity of attention and inattention, through his pattern of questioning, shapes the development of meaning in a medical interview may be found in Paget (1983).

Second, rather than applying a standard code-category system that abstracts and isolates pieces of talk from their contexts in the flow of speech, a unit of discourse has been developed that reflects the structure of an interview as a set of contingent utterances, namely, questions, responses, and assessment/questions.

Third, the function of this unit has been interpreted with reference to the particular meaning of the interview as an example of a clinical situation. The participants are not just any speakers, to be designated Speaker 1 and Speaker 2, but a patient and a physician. Thus, the fact that the speaker who opens and terminates each cycle of discourse is the physician is used as the basis for a specific interpretation of clinical practice, namely, that a structural unit of discourse embodies, maintains, and confirms the physician's control and dominance of the interview.

We may now move beyond this level of interpretation to the stage referred to earlier as "interruption." The particular patterning of form and content shown in the analysis documents and defines the interview as "unremarkable," a characterization that was made on intuitive grounds. The clear pattern suggests that the discourse expresses a particular "voice," to use Silverman and Torode's (1980) term. Since the interview is dominated by the physician, I will refer to this as the "voice of medicine."

The topic introduced by the patient in VII, her tiredness and difficulty sleeping, is in another voice; I will call it the "voice of the lifeworld." It is an interruption, or an attempted interruption, of the ongoing discourse being carried on in the "voice of medicine." It is of some interest that the patient's introduction of another voice occurs in response to the open-ended question: "How do you feel?" Except for his intitial question, this is the only open-ended question asked by the physician in this excerpt. In this instance, the second voice is suppressed; it does not lead to an opening of the discourse into a fuller and more mutual dialogue between the two voices. Rather, the physician reasserts the dominance of the voice of medicine through his response: "Because of the cough." Interruptions of the discourse and their effects will receive further attention in the following analyses.

It is instructive to examine in some detail the pattern of pauses and hesitations in the respective utterances of physician and patient. The findings of this analysis that pauses are not randomly distributed, but located systematically at certain points, particularly in the transitions between speakers, reinforces the argument made earlier about the importance of including such details of speech in transcripts. If we look at the cycle transition points (that is, from I–II, II–III, etc., that the physician controls through his utterance with a dual function—terminating the previous cycle with a post-response assessment and initiating the new cycle with a question), we find a relatively consistent pattern. The physician either breaks into the patient's statement before she has completed it, thus terminating her statement with his own comment—an "Okay" or "hm hm"—as in I–II, II–III, IV–V, and V–VI, or he takes his next turn without pause as soon as the patient finishes, as in III–IV, VI–VII, and VII–VIII. Often, the assessment-terminating part of his utterance is followed by a pause, filled or unfilled, before the question that begins the next cycle, as in the utterances marking the beginnings of cycles II, III, IV, and VI.

It is worth noting that of the three cycles that vary from this pause pattern, two are questions about general health (VII and VIII), which differ significantly from the earlier specific symptom questions. The other utterance that deviates from this pattern begins in V; this is the only cycle-transition utterance that does not include an explicit assessment such as "Okay," "hm hm," or "alright." However, an alternative specification of cycle IV boundaries would bring this utterance into conformity with the general pattern. In this case, we could define the termination of the cycle with the physician's "hm hm" that breaks into the patient's response. The usual pause between his assessment and the next question, both part of his single utterance, is filled by the patient's continuation of her response. This alternative structure is marked on the transcript in dashed lines and numbered as IV and IV'. This reformulation makes more sense, in part because it fits the general pattern, but also because the patient has already answered the question when he offers his assessment. What she says after his "hm hm" is extra, or "surplus," and he appears to treat it as irrelevant by breaking in before she completes her statement and ignoring it, since he makes no assessment and goes immediately on to his next question. In summary, with this alternative description, all but two of the physician's utterances at these transition points have the same structure: assessment response, pause, new question. The two utterances that vary from this, at the beginnings of VII and VIII, differ in the topic that they introduce; this may turn out to be an important formal characteristic that distinguishes them from symptom questions.

These pauses, systematically located between the physician's assessment of the patient's response and his next question, appear to serve a specific function; a preliminary interpretation may be proposed that they mark the termination of one cycle of discourse and are the physician's way of making clear to the patient that her response is "adequate" and that nothing more need be or should be said on the topic. At the same time, they prepare the patient to expect a next question beginning a new cycle. On the basis of this interpretation, the pause is assigned to the physician, it "belongs" in his utterance and is not simply a period of silence that might be filled by either speaker. This is yet another, and subtle, way in which the physician controls the flow of the interview.

It is evident from the transcript that pauses and hesitations occur more frequently in the patient's utterances than in the physician's. Two different patterns of pauses are apparent in the patient's responses although neither of them is as clear as the pattern of pauses in the physician's utterances.

In the first type, a brief pause precedes the patient's response to a question. We find this in four of the seven cycles following the first: II, III, V, and VII. In two of these cycles, V and VII, the physician asks further questions. If we look at patient responses to all ten of his questions in this excerpt, we find the pause-response pattern in five of them. If we look closely at the five instances where there appears to be a direct response to his question, not preceded by a pause, we find only two with what might be called a simple response structure: the patient's last utterance in V, "There's been nothing on the hankerchief," and her "No" in VI. In other instances, with no initial pause, the patient either breaks off the beginning of her response and then reformulates her answer, as in IV and the second question in VII, or gives a double answer, as in VIII.

There is a second pattern of pauses in the patient's utterances that is worth noting. Although her initial and within-utterance pauses both tend to be short, 0.4–0.6 seconds, three responses are preceded by markedly longer pauses; each of these also includes a non-lexical filler such as "uhm" or "uh:m." They are responses to the initial question in III (preceded by a pause of 1.2"); to the second question in V (1.3"); and to the initial question in VII (1.8"). It appears that these questions require more thought and that the time required for the patient to formulate an adequate answer is reflected in the pause length. She has to think more about her answers to questions about her ears, the color of the nasal discharge, how she feels than about the presence of fever, type of cough, and so on.

In addition, there is a detectable sequential pattern in the patient's responses. If we group the cycles together in clusters, II–IV, the three questions in V, and VI–VIII, then it appears that the first response is preceded by a short pause, the second by a long pause, and the third by no pause. Thus, in the sequence of responses to physician questions in II, III, and IV we find responses preceded by pause lengths of 0.6, 1.2″ with a nonlexical, and 0.0, respectively; in the sequence of three questions in V, we find 0.4, 1.3″ with a nonlexical, and 0.0. The sequence from VI–VIII shows some variation, but the long pause is still in second slot: 0.0, 1.8″ with a nonlexical, and two successive responses with 0.0 pauses.

This pattern or quasi-pattern of pause lengths in the sequence of patient responses is of sufficient interest to merit a tentative interpretation of its source. We begin with a general conversational norm observed of avoiding gaps between turns (see Sacks, Schegloff, & Jefferson, 1974). Speakers tend to take their turns as soon as the other speaker has finished, with no pause at all, or a minimal one. It has been proposed that this short interval depends on the second speaker knowing when the first speaker will finish. To serve this function, the trajectory of a first utterance, particularly in adjacency pairs such as questions and answers, is designed to signal the first speaker's turn completion point. The physician tends to follow the no-gap rule in his assessments of patient responses. In some instances, he breaks in while the patient is speaking without waiting for a normal completion point, thus indicating that the response is complete for his purposes. The patient's situation is quite different. In a medical interview, patients do not know what next question to expect or whether their initial answer will be treated as adequate. If the physician provides some "help" in alerting the patient to the topic of the question and its potential completion point, then the patient is able to anticipate more easily when to answer and to what topic the answer should refer. If the physician does not provide help of this kind, then the disconnected questions, one following another without apparent reason, make it difficult for the patient to maintain the conversational flow.

The sequence from II–IV provides a good example with some support for this line of speculation. The physician's first question, "Any fever?" has no prior reference and comes with no helpful signals, but would be recognized by a patient as appropriate and relevant. The response is preceded by a moderately short pause of 0.6″. His next question, "How bout your ears?" does not "follow" from her response, and in fact, is preceded by his interruption of her response. This is followed by a relatively long pause of 1.2″ with a non-lexical embedded in it. His third question, "Now this uh cough what are you producing anything or is it a dry cough?" (in IV), however, refers back to the cough symptom the patient mentioned earlier and is a relatively long utterance which gives her time to think, and has the form of a disjunctive question which gives her two specific alternatives to choose for her answer. The patient responds to this question without an initial pause. Other instances will not be examined in detail as they provide no strong counter evidence.

I am suggesting that the length of initial pauses in the patient's responses is directly related to the degree to which the physician's successive questions are meaningfully related to previous responses or to the general topic under discussion. Such continuity of meaning tends to be present in ordinary conversation where speakers are mutually attentive and jointly engaged in developing the "topic" of their talk. In medical interviews, where the physician controls the flow of topics, the relationship between speakers and their utterances is more variable. When there is a clear relationship in the sense that the physician's question is explicitly tied to the patient's response or to his own previous question, the patient responds immediately or with minimal pause. When the topic in his next question is not connected to her response, her pre-utterance pause before responding is longer, reflecting the increased time required to formulate an appropriate response.

Finally, the syntactic structure of the physician's questions is worth noting since it reflects his control of the interview at another level. In this excerpt, there are 11 instances where the physician terminates his turn with a question. Excluding his opening question and his clarification question, "What?", in V, which seem to function differently, five of the remaining nine questions are Yes/No in structure, and one is Polar/Disjunctive, that is, a pair of alternative answers is provided in the question for the patient to choose between. Another, in V, is a restricted Wh- question:

"What color is it?" A moderately open How- question is found in III: "How bout your ears?" and an open How- question in VI: "How do you feel?" Overall, in seven of these nine questions, the patient's response is restricted by the form of the question. Thus, in addition to controlling the turn-taking system and initiating topics for discussion, the physician also controls the interview through the form of the questions he asks.

Findings from this analysis of one "unremarkable" interview will be summarized at this point. They provide a characterization, albeit tentative and preliminary, of normal and routine clinical practice, and can be used as a framework for comparing and contrasting analyses of other interviews.

First, the basic structural unit of a medical interview is a linked set of three utterances: a physician's opening question, a patient's response, and the physician's response to the patient which usually, but not always, begins with an assessment followed by a second question. The second utterance of the physician serves the dual function of terminating the first unit, or cycle, and initiating the next. In this way, the separate units are connected together to form the continuous discourse of the interview.

The primary discourse function of the basic structure is that it permits the physician to control the development of the interview. His control is assured by his position as both first and last speaker in each cycle, which allows him to control the turn-taking system and the sequential organization of the interview. This structure of dominance is reinforced by the content of the physician's assessments and questions that he asks, which selectively attend to or ignore particulars of the patient's responses. The physician's dominance is expressed at still another level through the syntactic structure of his questions. These tend to be restrictive closed-end questions, which limit the range of relevance for patient responses. At all these levels, the focus of relevance, that is, of appropriate meaning, is on medically relevant material, as is defined by the physician.

Within utterances, two patterns of pauses were identified that are consistent with the overall structure and its functions. Typically, in physician utterances there is a pause between the assessment and the next question. This serves to mark the termination of the prior unit and the initiation of the next one. The length of initial pauses in patient responses appears to depend on the location of a cycle wihin a sequence of cycles. Patient utterances in the first cycle of a series are preceded by a short pause, in the second cycle by a long pause, and in the third cycle by no pause. This seems to be related to the degree of disjunction between successive physician questions and whether or not he "helps" the patient prepare for a response by making his next question relevant to her prior response.

Finally, all the features and functions of this unit of discourse have been brought together under a general analytic category referred to as the "voice of medicine." The physician's control of the interview through the structure of turn-taking and through the form and content of his questions expresses the normative order of medicine. The dominance of this voice produces our intuitive impression of the interview as an instance of normal clinical practice, that is, as unremarkable. Patients may attempt to interrupt the dominant voice by speaking in the "voice of the lifeworld." This alternative voice may be suppressed, as it was in this interview, or may open up the interview to a fuller dialogue between voices. Relationships between the two voices will be explored further in this and following chapters.

Medical History (W:02. 013)

The second excerpt for analysis (Transcript 3.2) is also taken from the beginning of an interview. From the content and sequence of his questions, it appears that the physician is following a form, such as the medical history section of an insurance application. The aim of this analysis will be to determine whether the structure and flow of a different type of "unremarkable" interview is similar to the first.

One strong similarity is immediately apparent. Similar to the first interview, this one consists of a series of connected cycles, each with the same structure that was found before: physician question, patient response, physician question. The function of the second physician question is also the same, that is, it serves both to terminate the first cycle and intitiate the next one. The excerpt contains nine full cycles and the beginning of a tenth. Only one of these cycles (II) is expanded internally; all the others have a simple structure.

The second feature to note is that, with the exception of the transition turn between I and II, the physician does not offer explicit assessments prior to his next questions. Moreover, I differs

Transcript 3.2

W:02.013

I   001 D   No:w . and u:uh .... lemme see ....

      002   .... and your name sir.

      003 P   Albert Morrison.

II   004 D   Okay

      005   Albert urgh:h .... (that does .. that's for

II′   006   memos) .... *Okay Albert* u::h .... Have there any

      007   cases of tuberculosis diabetes (acantees) suicide among

      008   your relatives.

      009 P   (h) ...... (h) My father had tuberculosis

      010   oh:h .... tst . twenty ohgee twenty five thirty

      011   years ago he in the hospital .... he was there

      012   two years.

II″   013 D   Twenty five years ago herng:h?

      014 P   .... Oh

      015   maybe longer than that. (h) I was a little boy. Twenty

      016   five- Yeah I'd say twenty five years ago.

                   [

III   017 D   (...)   .... Have

      018   you (within) the last ten years been intimately associated

      019   with anyone having tuberculosis?

      020 P   .... No.

IV   021 D   Have you ever

      022   consulted a doctor suffered from any illnesses or diseases

      023   of the brain or the nervous system.

      024 P   No.

V   025 D   Heart blood

      026   vessels or lungs?

      027 P   N:no.

VI   028 D   Stomach or intestines.

      029 P   No.

VII   030 D   Skin

      031   glands (nurr) your *eyes*?

      032 P   No.

VIII   033 D   Have you ever had rheumatism

      034   bone disease or syphillis.

| | 035 | P | No. |

IX
- 036 D Have you ever seen a doctor
- 037 suffered from any illness or disease not included in
- 038 the above questions other than for routine colds.
- 039 P No.

X
- 040 D ...... (h) Now name all the doctors who have treated
- 041 you in the last three years.

(1′2″)

from the other cycles in that it is a request for the patient's name and is preparatory rather than part of the interview itself. Although lack of explicit assessments may have other functions in other contexts, in this interview it suggests a level of nonresponsiveness to the patient's responses and, therefore, appears to mark a greater degree of impersonality and distance than was present in the first interview. Another marker of impersonality is the physician's opening question, "and your name sir," which comes after some initial hesitations. Clearly, the man in his office is not one of the physician's patients; they have not met before.

Nonetheless, the formality of the request is unusual. The physician does not introduce himself, nor does he inquire into or refer to the reasons for their meeting. His request for the patient's name is in the form that we might expect from an official in a bureaucratic setting. The "sir" does not signal deference, but an impersonal requirement that a name be recorded on a form. The intent of the request is to elicit the patient's name, and the patient clearly responds with his first and last name in compliance with the physician's request.

There is an impression of routinization in these exchanges resulting from several features. One is the type of physician question; he runs together disparate items as if they had no separate meaning, and indeed, as if none of them had any particular significance. For example, his questions clump together "tuberculosis, diabetes, (acantees), suicide," "heart blood vessels or lungs," "stomach or intestines," "skin glands (nurr) your eyes," and "rheumatism bone disease or syphilis." Some of these are strange combinations, but their strangeness goes unremarked by both physician and patient. Another routinizing feature is that the patient's responses, after cycle II, are all unexpanded "No" answers. Except in one instance, there are no pauses between the patient's responses and physician's questions, no attention markers by the physician, and no explicit assessments. These omissions all contribute to the sense of routine impersonality.

These various features make a strong case for inferring that the physician is filling out a form, probably an insurance application. That is, he is following the questions as they would appear on the form. A further inference is that although the assessments are unstated, they are not entirely absent. That is, it seems probable that the physician could be recording the patient's answers on the form as check marks in the boxes provided, and that this is visible and apparent in the interview situation thereby reducing the need for an explicit verbal assessment by the physician.

The patient's response to the first question in cycle II is relatively extensive and leads into a expanded cycle with an additional physician question. The patient hesitates before answering the complex question about "any cases of tuberculosis diabetes (acantees) suicide among your relatives." He begins by specifying "My father had tuberculosis" and then states when and how long his father had been in a hospital. The patient's response to the next question, in cycle III, is an unexpanded "No" preceded by a brief pause. From that point on, his successive "No" responses follow the physician's questions without pause. In a sense, he appears to have "learned" to give quick, short answers that do not elicit extended physician responses as resulted with his first answer when he took the question more seriously than was warranted by the task at hand. Filling out this form, the physician seems to be saying, through his own pattern of rapid questioning and nonassessment, that this is not a regular medical examination, therefore, medical details are not necessary. This is another way in which the physician creates a sense that their interaction is relatively impersonal, restricted in meaning, and distant from what they might otherwise share for a serious concern about health and illness.

The physician reinforces this pattern of restricted and unexpanded responses by his rapid pattern of questioning. Except in two instances, there are no delays between the patient's response and the next physician question. One of the exceptions, the transition between cycles IX and X, marks a shift in topic; it is as if one section of the form has been completed. This question will require a different type of answer; giving a list of names.

The other exception to physician questions without initial pauses is the more complicated transition question from cycle II to III. After an aborted attempt to interrupt the patient, the physician pauses before his next question: "..... Have you (within) the last ten years been intimately associated with anyone having tuberculosis?" It is possible to consider this as an expansion of II rather than the initiation of a new cycle. The physician reformulates his opening question to provide a more specific range of relevance (a period of 10 years), and to increase the degree of intimate association in order to elicit a more appropriate and limited response. Clearly, this question is doing more work than the straightforward questions that enumerate illnesses. Either the effort to reformulate the question in a more precise way or the possibility that it is an actual shift in the type of question on the questionnaire might account for the hesitation.

In general, this series of questions does not have the aim of those in the previous diagnostic interview. The physician is not trying to clarify the significance of a particular symptom; he is simply recording features of a medical history.

Keeping all these differences in mind, it is still evident that the general form of an assessment interview is preserved in the basic unit structures and in the ways they are linked together. Thus, in its structure, it is similar to the first unremarkable interview in which this structure functions to maintain the physician's control of the interview. In addition, there are specific ways in which this structure is realized that make this interview more impersonal, more cut-and-dried, and more objectified than the first one.

Despite differences in particular features of this series of exchanges, the similarity between this interview and the earlier one in basic structure and in the physician's control of the organization and meaning of the discourse indicate that we are again in the presence of the "voice of medicine." It might be useful to think of this voice as including several dialects or codes; the two unremarkable interviews represent two such dialects that vary in degree of formality.[6] In this instance, the physician is serving other interests, those of an insurance company. A physician's professional expertise is routinely called upon in a variety of situations where an individual's eligibility for a job, or the legitimacy of a

---

[6] For an interesting discussion of the features of different styles within the same language that vary in formality see Joos (1961).

person's claim for compensation or for exemption from obligations may legally and/or institutionally require determination of his/her "health" status (Waitzkin & Waterman, 1974). This requirement and the role of the physician as the official and legitimate "certifier" of competence or disability overlays, but does not displace, the standard clinical task. However, it restricts the physician and leads to a mode of discourse that is unidimensional and impersonal. Metaphorically speaking, the voice of medicine loses some of the resonance that exists in any direct discourse, even one that is as narrowly focused as a standard diagnostic interview.

There is one point in this interview, as we found in the earlier one, where the patient intrudes with the "voice of the lifeworld," although it is somewhat muted. It appears in the patient's extended response to the physician's first question in cycle II. He reports not only that his father had tuberculosis, but how long ago, how long he was hospitalized, and that he was a "little boy" at the time. This is certainly not a strong voice, but it includes surplus information not required for an adequate answer to the question. These elements are provided through additional or tag comments to the patient's first answer. Both the addition of surplus content and its placement are signs of another voice. This creates "trouble," similar to that encountered earlier when a new voice entered. There is a break in the physician's fluency of speech; his only interruption of the patient and his one pause preceding a question occur here. Nonetheless, the physician quickly reintroduces the voice of medicine by his next question, noted earlier, in which he restricts the time period and specifies an "intimate" association. This question instructs the patient as to what is required and from this point on he limits his answers to "No" without providing additional information.

The Interruption of Clinical Discourse

The structure of clinical discourse has been explicated through analyses of two unremarkable interviews. The basic three-part unit of such discourse and the ways in which these units are linked together has been described, as well as the functions served by this structure—the physician's control of organization and meaning. I referred to this patterned relationship between structure and function as the "voice of medicine," and suggested that it expressed the normative order of medicine and clinical practice. This voice provides a baseline against which to compare other medical interviews that depart in some way from normal and routine practice.

Some preliminary comparisons have already been made. In each of these unremarkable interviews the patient interrupted the flow of the discourse by introducing the "voice of the lifeworld." In both instances, the new voice was quickly silenced and the physician reasserted his dominance and the singularity of the clinical perspective. In the following interview, the patient makes more of an effort to sustain an alternative voice. Examining how the patient does this and how the physician responds will extend our understanding of the specific features and functions of medical interviews and will also alert us to problems that develop when there are departures from normal and routine clinical work. This discussion will also bring forward an issue that will be central to later analyses; the struggle between the voices of medicine and of the lifeworld.

Symptom and Lifeworld Context: Negotiation of Meaning (W: 13.121/01)

The patient is a 26-year-old woman with stomach pains, which she describes as a sour stomach beginning several weeks prior to this medical visit. The excerpt (Transcript 3.3) begins about 3½ minutes into the interview, preceded by a review of her history of peptic ulcers in childhood and the time and circumstances of the present complaint.

In the excerpt, the first four cycles and the beginning of the fifth are similar in structure to the interviews analyzed earlier. Each one begins with the physician's question about the symptom. This is followed by a response from the patient, sometimes preceded by a pause, and is terminated by the physician's next question. His question is sometimes preceded by an assessment, which then initiates the next cycle.

Two other features of the first four cycles may be noted. Although there are occasional pauses prior to the patient's responses and some false starts as she appears to search for an appropriate answer, there are few within-utterance pauses and those that occur

Transcript 3.3

W:13.121/01

```
    ┌ 001 D  Hm hm .... Now what do you mean by a sour stomach?
  I │  002 P  ................. What's a sour stomach? A heartburn
    │  003     like a heartburn or something.
    │                           [
    └
    ┌ 004 D                          Does it burn over here?
 II │  005 P                                              Yea:h.
    │  006     It li- I think- I think it like- If you take a needle
    │  007     and stick ya right .... there's a pain right here ..
    │                    [         [                    [
    │  008 D             Hm hm Hm hm              Hm hm
    │  009 P  and and then it goes from here on this side to this side.
    └ 010 D  Hm hm Does it go into the back?
    ┌                      [
III │  011 P              It's a:ll up here. No. It's all right
    │  012     up here in the front.
    └          [
    ┌ 013 D  Yeah              And when do you get that?
 IV │  014 P                                         ........
    └ 015     .......... Wel:l when I eat something wrong.
  V ┌ 016 D                                      How- How
 V' │ 017     soon after you eat it?
    │ 018 P              ........................ Wel:l
    │ 019     ...... probably an hour .... maybe less.
    │                                 [
V'' │ 020 D                            About an hour?
    │ 021 P  Maybe less ............ I've cheated and I've been
    │ 022     drinking which I shouldn't have done.
    └ 023 D                                    ..........
    ┌ 024     Does drinking making it worse?
 VI │          [
    │ 025 P  (...)                         Ho ho uh ooh Yes. ....
    │ 026     ...... Especially the carbonation and the alcohol.
    └ 027 D  ........ Hm hm ........ How much do you drink?
VII ┌ 028 P                                    ......
VII'│ 029     ................ I don't know. .. Enough to make me
```

	030		go to sleep at night .... and that's quite a bit.
VII″	031	D	One or two drinks a day?
	032	P	O:h no no no humph it's (more
	033		like) ten. ...... at night.
			[
	034	D	How many drinks- a night.
	035	P	At night.
	036	D	.....
	037		..... Whaddya ta- What type of drinks? .... I (...)-
VIII			[
	038	P	Oh vodka
	039		.. yeah vodka and ginger ale.
	040	D	....
IX	041		...... How long have you been drinking that heavily?
IX′	042	P	.... Since I've been married.
	043	D	......
IX″	044		.. How long is that?
	045	P	(giggle..) Four years. (giggle)
	046		huh Well I started out with before then I was drinkin
	047		beer but u:m I had a job and I was .... ya know ......
	048		had more things on my mind and ya know I like- but
	049		since I got married I been in and out of jobs and
	050		everything so .... I- I have ta have something to
	051		go to sleep.
	052	D	...... Hm:m.
	053	P	.... I mean I'm not
	054		gonna- ...... It's either gonna be pills or it's
	055		gonna be .. alcohol .... and uh alcohol seems
	056		to satisfy me moren than pills do .... They don't
	057		seem to get strong enough .... pills that I have
	058		got I had- I do have Valium .... but they're two
	059		milligrams .... and that's supposed to
	060		quiet me down during the day but it doesn't.
	061	D	......
X	062		How often do you take them?

(1′47″)

are of short duration. For the physician, the pattern found earlier of a pause between assessment and question is occasionally present, but there are no false starts or pauses between the patient's responses and the physician's next questions. Again, there is a high degree of fluency in his speech.

The routine breaks down in cycle V. The patient's response to the physician's question with its false start includes a signal of trouble: "How- How soon after you eat it?" The patient's response is preceded by her longest pre-utterance pause (one of 2.5"), and contains two relatively long intra-utterance pauses. A major change comes in her next response, after restating her previous answer, "Maybe less," in response to his clarification question: "About an hour?" This physician question is treated as an internal expansion within V, although it might also be considered as beginning a new cycle, V'. Her answer, "Maybe less," is followed by a moderately long intra-utterance pause of 1.2", after which she introduces a new topic, her drinking.

This new topic comes in the form of a "tag" comment added to her answer to the physician's question and it has some features that mark it as different from what has previously been said. "....I've cheated and I've been drinking which I shouldn't have done." has a quality of intonation that is unusual when compared with her earlier responses. Those who have heard the tape recording easily recognize the difference and describe her speech as "teasing," "flirtatious," or "childish."

The physician's next question, which terminates V and initiates VI, is preceded by his first long pre-question hesitation: "..........Does drinking make it worse?" This is the first break in the fluency of his pattern of questioning. Further, he talks over the patient's attempt to say something more. His uncertainty, indicated by his pause, reflects two changes in the nature of the interview. The patient's comment introduces her drinking and, since this new topic is not in response to a direct question from the physician, it also shifts the control of the interview from physician to patient. I pointed out in earlier analyses that the basic structure of the medical interview, physician question-patient response-physician (assessment) question, permits the physician to control the form and content of the interview. As the "questioner," the physician controls the turn-taking structure and through the focus of his assessments and questions controls the development of meaning;

he defines what is and what is not relevant. By her tag comment, the patient has taken control both of form and meaning; she has introduced another voice.

With this tentative hypothesis that the normal structure of the medical interview has been interrupted and that as a result, the normal pattern of control has also been disrupted, we might expect to find evidence of: (a) other indicators of disruption and breakdown in the continuing exchange, and (b) efforts on the part of the physician to repair the disruption, to restore the normal structure, and to reassert the dominant voice of medicine.

The physician's pre-question hesitation after the patient introduces the new topic has already been noted as a sign of disruption, a change from his usual response timing: "........ Does drinking make it worse?" Similar and frequently longer pauses appear before all of his succeeding questions initiating new cycles at VII, VIII, IX, and X. The regularity of these pauses is quite striking, particularly when it is contrasted with the equally striking occurrence of no pauses preceding questions in cycles with a normal structure (I–IV).

Throughout the second half of this excerpt, from cycles VI–X, there is a continuing struggle between physician and patient to take control of the interview. The patient tries to maintain her control by restatements of the problem of drinking in her life situation exemplifying the voice of the lifeworld. The physician, on the other, persistently tries to reformulate the problem in narrower, more medically-relevant terms. For example, to his question, "How much do you drink?" (the transition between cycles VI and VII), she replies, after a long pause of 2.2″, "I don't know ... Enough to make me go to sleep at night .... and that's quite a bit." He persists with two further questions, within cycle VII, requesting the specific number of drinks. In this manner, the physician attempts to recapture control of the meaning of her account; he is excluding her meaning of the function of drinking in her life and focusing on "objective" measures of quantity.

The physician persists in this effort. To his question about how long she has been drinking heavily (IX), she responds "Since I've been married," again preceding her response with a long pause. But this is not considered an adequate or relevant answer from the physician's point of view and he asks for an actual, objective time, "How long is that?" Finally, in a relatively extended account in cycle IX, the patient talks about her drinking, of problems since her marriage, and her preference for alcohol over pills. There is much surplus information in her story to which the physician might respond. He chooses to attend selectively to that part of her account which is of clear medical relevance, the taking of pills, and asks again for a precise, objective, and quantitative answer, "How often do you take them?"

Another way to indicate that a significant change has taken place in the structure of the interview during the fifth cycle is to take note of the difficulty encountered in attempting to describe this interview in terms of the structural units found in the analyses of the first two interviews. Although I have marked the cycles of the interview in the same way, distinguishing the successive series of physician question-patient response-physician (assessment) question exchanges, there are problems in using this unit here. This structural unit assumes that an exchange is initiated by the physician's question and that the three-part exchange cycle is then terminated by the physician as he initiates the next cycle.

The problem may be seen in cycle V, at the point of the patient's comment about her drinking. This statement is not in response to a direct question; rather it is a statement introducing a new topic. The physician's next question refers to this new topic and he thus remains "in role." The reader will note that all of the physician's statements, except for his "Hm" assessments, are questions. The implicit function of questions remains which is to control the form and content of the interview, however in this instance, there is a break in the continuity of the physician's control. As an alternative structure to the one presented, we could ask whether a new cycle should begin with the patient's tag comment. If that were done, the physician's next question would be treated as a "response" to her statement, even though it is framed as a question. I'm not proposing an answer to the problem of structural analysis at this preliminary stage. However, I am suggesting that the change in the interview resulting from the patient's comment introduces problems for analysis. These problems provide another line of evidence for the assertion that there has been a breakdown in the normal structure of the clinical interview. These problems also suggest that a reconceptualization of clinical work may be required. This will be undertaken in the next chapter in which a reinterpretation of the interview will be proposed that alters the form of structural analysis.

Another potential indicator of a change in the structure of the interview, and a possible shift in control, is the location and presence of preutterance pauses. In the typical cycles beginning with physician questions, we often find a pause preceding the patient's response as in I, III, and the first part of V. Typically, the physician asks the next question with no turn-transition pause. This changes in the transition from V to VI when the physician pauses after the patient's introduction of the new topic of drinking. There are pauses preceding all of the physician's later cycle-initiating questions, and pauses also precede many of his intra-cycle expansion questions; for example, in IX. I am suggesting that another feature deserving further exploration as a possible marker of control of the interview is the shift in the location of pre-utterance pauses between speakers.

In this discussion, I have been using the occurrence of a noticeable change in the structure and flow of an interview to raise questions about how to analyze and understand the workings of medical interviews. The introduction of a new topic by the patient altered the routine pattern of the interview found in earlier "unremarkable" interviews. The features of physician and patient utterances varied in specific ways from those found earlier. These changes raised questions about which speaker was controlling the development of the interview, and hence controlling the development of meaning. The idea of "voices," and the distinction between the "voice of medicine" and the "voice of the lifeworld," was introduced to characterize alternative orders of meaning and the struggle between them. These issues will be explored in more detail in subsequent analyses.

Discussion

The aim of this chapter has been to develop concepts and methods for the analysis of discourse and to apply them to the study of medical interviews. Assumptions underlying the approach reflect the critique of past research, particularly of the mainstream tradition, on these problems. Several features of the approach adopted here can be singled out for summary comment.

First, interviews were selected for detailed analysis and discussion on the basis of an intuitive and preliminary understanding of them as typical and normal.[7] They were referred to as unremarkable since they appeared to fit general expectations of what happens in a medical interview. More specifically, patients and physicians talked about topics that we would expect them to talk about and in the ways that we would expect them to. Transcripts of these interviews included features of speech assumed to carry significance for how the discourse is organized, how it functions, and how it represents a particular normative order. The transcript notation system used allows for the textual representation of silences, speech overlaps, insertion comments, and certain vocalizations and speech stresses, as well as for the organization of successive utterances by the two speakers into discourse units and the chaining together of these units into a series.

Analysis of these transcripts led to the discovery of a unit of discourse consisting of a three-part utterance sequence: physician question-patient response-physician (assessment) next question. The physician's second question served both to terminate the first unit and initiate the second, and produced a connected series of such cycles that constituted the interview. I noted earlier that the research stage of interpretation referred essentially to the function of structural features of the discourse. The preliminary interpretation proposed here is that this structural unit of discourse both permits and sustains the physician's control of the interview. Further, detailed analyses of the types of questions asked by physicians and their selective attention to certain content led to the conclusion that they control the content as well as the structural organization of the interview. Since this interpretation is based on an analysis of unremarkable interviews, I argued that the structure and function of this unit of discourse represented normal and typical clinical practice.

A new analytic category was introduced to characterize this complex unity of structure and function. It was referred to as the "voice of medicine"—the notion that a particular normative order was represented in the discourse. In this instance, the normative order was the perspective of medicine, the biomedical model.[8] Further analyses revealed that the "voice of the lifeworld" oc-

---

[7] See Footnote 1 for a description of the sample of interviews from which these were selected.

[8] The assumptions of the biomedical model are outlined and examined critically in Mishler (1981).

casionally found expression. Patients sometimes talked about problems in their lives that were related to or resulted from their symptoms or illnesses. The meanings expressed in this voice differed from those framed within the biomedical perspective and physicians tended to treat this material as nonmedically relevant. In a typical interview, this other voice was quickly suppressed and the physician restored the voice of medicine to its position of dominance in the discourse. There were instances, however, where there was a struggle between the voices for control. This was associated with disruption of the usual flow of the interview.

These analyses are a first level of interpretation. In the next chapter, the assumptions of this approach will be subjected to the strategy of interruption analysis. This new series of analyses will extend, deepen, and change our understanding of clinical practice.

Appendix to Chapter 3: Typescript Notation

Representing speech as written text is a form of translation in which sounds are transformed into a visual display. No one true transcription is possible and different transcriptions must be expected. Rather than attempting to construct a standard "best" transcript, my more limited aim has been to achieve a high degree of isomorphism between those features of speech that are considered significant for the investigation at hand and the ways in which the text is marked and arranged. Any notation system used to describe speech incorporates a model of language. In the notation system used here, particular attention is paid to the temporal sequencing of speakers, that is, when they take their turns relative to the other speaker's utterance, and to silences both within and between utterances. There is less attention to intonation, volume, pacing, or other features of the quality of speech.

1. Line Number	001 002 ... 999	
	Typescript lines are numbered sequentially from the first line in an excerpt.	
2. Speaker	D P	
	D is doctor, P is patient. Speaker is noted at the first line of an utterance and at overlap points.	

3. Turn/Utterance
   Location   Each new turn, that is, the beginnings of utterances by speakers in a sequence, starts at that point on the transcript line that corresponds to the temporal relationship of the utterance to the prior one. When there is no gap or overlap between speakers, the second utterance begins one space over on the next transcript line; gaps and overlaps are indicated by appropriate markers. Turn beginnings are not shifted back to the left hand margin unless the prior utterance ends at the end of a transcript line

4. Overlap   [

   If a speaker begins to talk while the other is still talking, the point of beginning overlap is marked by a bracket [between the lines.

5. Silence   ....

   Silences within speaker utterances and between speakers are marked by a series of dots; each dot represents one-tenth (0.1) of a second. These silences are assigned to the next speaker if they occur between speakers, that is, they are given the meaning of a pre-utterance pause.

6. Unclarity   (cold)/(...)

   Where a word(s) is heard but remains unclear, it is included in parentheses; if there are speaking sounds that are unintelligible, this is noted as dots within parentheses.

7. Speech Features   ?/.

   Punctuation marks are used when intonation clearly marks the utterance as a question or as the end of a sentence.

   :

   If a word is stretched, this is marked by a colon as in "Wel:l".

   -

   If speaker breaks off in the middle of a word or phrase, this is marked by a hyphen -, as in "haven't felt like-".

   (h)

Intake of breath either in a pause or at the beginning of a word.

h

Indicates laughter within an utterance.

—

Underline is used if there is a marked increase in loudness and/or emphasis. (Italics in text.)

8. Discourse Cycles

$$
\text{I}\begin{cases} \text{D} \\ \text{P} \\ \text{D} \end{cases}
$$

Connected exchanges between speakers that form a unit of discourse, as this has been defined in this study, are connected and numbered in the margin. Subcycles within these larger units that could be treated as separate cycles are connected by dashed lines, and numbered with single or double quotation marks.

CHAPTER 4

Interrupting the Voice of Medicine: A Radical Analysis

Introduction

The analyses in the preceding chapter demonstrated a variety of ways in which physicians control the structure and content of medical interviews. Close examination of a series of unremarkable interviews revealed how physicians' questions—by their placement in the discourse, by their form, and by their selective focus of attention—serve this function of control. Further, our sense of the coherence and continuity of such interviews, our recognition of them as instances of sustained and extended patient-physician discourse, depends on how separate units of discourse are linked together through the dual functions of physicians' questions, which terminate one cycle and initiate the next. Physicians' control of structure is matched by their control of content. The relevance and appropriateness of information is defined through what physicians choose to attend to and ask about. This bounded domain of relevance is summarized as the voice of medicine. Occasionally, the flow of the interview is "interrupted" by the "voice of the lifeworld" when patients refer to the personal and social contexts of their problems. Physicians rapidly repair such disruptions and reassert the voice of medicine.

These findings and interpretations provide the point of departure for a new set of analyses. Briefly, the present chapter begins by turning these earlier findings into an object of inquiry. A reexamination of the previous analysis is undertaken that includes a critique of its assumptions, the development and application of a new mode of analysis, and, finally, an alternative interpretation of the discourse of medical interviews.

This is an unusual way for an investigation to proceed, therefore it requires some preliminary comment. Essentially, I am pursuing and extending the research strategy referred to earlier as interruption analysis or critical reflection. Up to this point, the approach has shown how conflict between the medicine and lifeworld voices represented in patient-physician talk results in certain disturbances in the otherwise smooth flow and organization of discourse. The notion of interruption was restricted to the intrusion of the voice of the lifeworld into the medical interview causing speech hesitations and disruptions in turn-taking. This approach will now be applied in a more radical way, interrupting my own analyses. I hope to demonstrate that the process of critical reflection leads to a deeper, more adequate and more comprehensive understanding of how medical interviews work as particular types of discourse, of the different structures of meaning expressed in the voices of the lifeworld and of medicine, and of the broader social significance of the conflict between the two voices.

The analysis presented in this chapter moves progressively through several steps. It begins by questioning the assumptions and procedures of the earlier analyses, on which the findings of physician control and dominance of the voice of medicine depended. An exploration is undertaken of how to make sense of medical interviews if patients and their accounts are placed at the center of the discourse. This inverts the earlier analysis in which physicians were the central figures. As will be seen, this shift in emphasis leads to a reformulation of the voices of the lifeworld and of medicine, as well as to new transcription rules so that transcripts more closely represent this new sense of the interview. More precise descriptions of the two voices are developed that reveal their underlying structures of meaning and the ways that they interpenetrate in the discourse.

On the basis of these analyses a new interpretation is proposed: discontinuity replaces coherence as the central identifying feature of the interview and the struggle between voices, rather than the dominance of one voice, shapes the discourse. Finally, this revised interpretation of medical interviews is placed in a more general theoretical and social perspective. Specifically, the concept of voices is linked to Schutz' (1962) formulation of provinces of meaning and to the contrast between the scientific attitude and the attitude of everyday life. The implications of these relationships are further developed by applying Habermas' (1970) distinction between symbolic and purposive-rational action and his analysis of the conflict between their respective modes of consciousness, that of everyday life, and the technocratic consciousness.

Critique: Interruption of Earlier Analyses

In Chapter 3, I presented a framework for analyzing medical interviews as a type of discourse. Applying this framework to examples of unremarkable interviews, the structure of routine and normative medical practice was revealed as a linked series of physician question-patient response-physician assessment/question cycles. I argued that through this structure physicians maintained control of the organization and meaning of such interviews. Evidence of this pattern of control was found at various levels of language. I termed this form of discourse the "voice of medicine" and showed how it might be interrupted by patients speaking in the "voice of the lifeworld."

Although these findings might be viewed as implicit criticism of medical practice by conveying an image of physician coerciveness and dominance, there is an important sense in which the analysis itself remains within the voice of medicine. The salience of the voice of medicine in the analysis, the findings of physician dominance and control, the description of the patient's lifeworld concerns as "interruptions"—all these ways of formulating and analyzing the structure of the discourse and its problems function to maintain and reaffirm the dominance of the medical voice. In other words, the analysis remains confined within the phenomenon. It does not question the assumptions of the voice of medicine. In the end, the power of medicine and the dominant role of the physician are intact and untouched.[1]

---

[1] My efforts to reexamine the assumptions of the first series of analyses of unremarkable interviews was prompted by Tracy Paget's cogent observation that they left the power and dominance of the physician intact. Her critical reflection on my analysis had fruitful consequences and is gratefully acknowledged.

If we wish to break free of the voice of medicine, to open up new perspectives that would help us understand how to change a pattern of coercive medical care to more humane practice, then we have to begin again in a different way. In order to do this, the analysis must be inverted; the relations between the voices of medicine and the lifeworld must be reversed. In this way, the voice of medicine may be understood as an interruption of the voice of the lifeworld.

An example may clarify these issues. Earlier, in examining the excerpt in which the patient interrupted the discourse by introducing her drinking problem,[2] I pointed out that in the way she did this, she moved outside the constraints of the physician's definition of medically-relevant information. The patient persisted in her efforts to describe the functional significance of her problem in her lifeworld; the physician persisted in asking objective questions about time and quantity. I interpreted the effect of this discordance of "voices" as a disruption in the fluent flow of the interview, and used as evidence for this interpretation the hesitations and false starts found in the physician's speech at this point. I also remarked that this sequence created problems for the analysis since it was unclear whether these exchanges could be described adequately by the proposed structural unit of discourse. Another way in which the dominance of the medical voice was implicitly incorporated into the analysis was by my reference to the patient's interruption of the discourse as a "tag" comment.

In these various ways, the analysis relied upon and accepted the dominance of the physician. More specifically, the analysis did not "prove" or demonstrate that physicians were dominant, but the finding itself depended upon an underlying "silent" assumption of the physician's dominance. Thus, in this type of analysis, the voice of medicine was treated as the norm from which the patient deviated, the patient was portrayed as disrupting the "normal" basic structure of the medical interview, and her statement of her lifeworld problem was downgraded in meaning and subordinated to the "primary" medical content of the interview. This critical reexamination, or interruption, of the assumptions underlying the previous analysis and interpretation illustrates concretely the meaning of my earlier statement that the analysis

---

[2] See Transcript 3.3 in Chapter 3.

is confined within and reaffirms the dominance of the voice of medicine.

Let us begin with a different assumption, that the patient's account is primary. The patient has a story to tell; its theme is a lifeworld problem. In telling her story, she is interrupted by the physician speaking in the voice of medicine. The excerpt selected begins with the physician's question. Selecting the physician as the initiator of the sequence shows that the assumption of physician dominance entered into the analysis even at the first level of description.

In order to develop a new analysis, we must go back to that point in the interview where the patient begins her account. If we look at the fuller transcript of the interview from the beginning, we find that the patient's first explicit mention of her symptom as a "sour stomach" occurs early on (at 044),[3] after some initial exchanges about her medical history of ulcers when she was 9 to 13 years of age. (The transcript is appended to this chapter.)

In response to the physician's question about when her childhood ulcers appeared, one when she was 9 and another a few years later, the patient first uses the term "sour stomach."

```
040 D  And how did- how did the ulcers present. What uh- What happened?
       ...... Just pain or uh
    P                          It's a- Wel:l
       . ye:ah . pa- lot- lots and lots of pain sour stomach
    D                                                    Hm hm
```

This exchange is in the context of a series of medical history questions. The physician has focused on ulcers in childhood, a problem he has found on her chart.

```
018 D  .......... Okay now you've had . acccording to this thing ....................
       uh:m .................... you haven- you had an ulcer at age *nine*?
```

The physician's intonation expresses some disbelief at the age recorded in the chart.

The exchanges that follow this question could be charted, as

---

[3] Numbers cited with quoted utterances in the text, such as (044), refer to transcript lines in the interview appended to this chapter. When the quoted statement refers to more than one line, the number is the line on which it begins.

was done earlier, as a set of cycles initiated and linked by physician questions. In such an analysis, we might find that the patient occasionally interrupts the voice of medicine by reporting, for example, that her doctor had been "shocked to death" (036) by the fact that a girl so young had two ulcers. However, my aim is to interrupt the previous analysis, to turn it on its head, and to make the voice of the lifeworld central so that the voice of medicine will be seen as the interruption. To do this, we must begin with the patient's story.

It begins with her first response to the physician's opening comment that she had been sent up from the screening clinic. The patient corrects him by asserting that she "was sent up here from uh - from neurology really," and provides the reason: "........ because I told them-...... I told them what my symptoms were .... and uh they said okay ...... we'll get you up there" (007). But "first," apparently before going to the clinic, she had seen her own doctor who put her on a diet, gave her pills, and ordered her to have X-rays taken before she returned to him. In beginning her story, the patient offers an account of why she has come to the physician. She was sent to him to have a diagnostic examination that would, in particular, include X-rays because of "symptoms," as yet unspecified.

When we return to the physician's next utterance, in which he refers to her ulcer at age 9, we find that although he briefly acknowledges her account through his opening "Okay" (018), he does not refer to or comment on any of its particular elements. Nor, does he ask her to continue or elaborate her story. This is the first type of interruption by the physician. We might gloss it initially as interruption by inattention. It is not simply passive, however, but is combined with a more active mode; the physician's introduction of another story, her childhood ulcers. The potential link between these two juxtaposed stories is provided by the patient's medical chart or record, "according to that thing," that is, by a document constructed with reference to a system of medical relevances. Compared to an apparent vagueness and lack of specificity in the patient's account, the physician becomes precise. The patient does not provide particulars; she refers over the course of her initial account to: "my symptoms," "up there," "my doctor," "a diet," "some pills," "in there," and "X-rays." In contrast, the physician refers specifically to "an ulcer at age *nine?*"

At a later point, I will examine the structure of the patient's story in some detail; here, a summary will serve to provide an overall sense of what she is trying to say and the difficulties she encounters. Her story has a certain order of complexity, but it is neither obscure nor difficult to understand. Nonetheless, a coherent paraphrase requires a fair amount of reconstruction and rearrangement of the text since her story emerges as a series of fragments. This fragmentation results from the physician's mode of questioning in which he shifts from one topic to another without explicitly connecting them. The patient, however, does provide connections that allow for the following summary restatement of her story as she develops and expresses it in the interview:

> Starting a few weeks ago, in January, I began to have the following symptoms: sour stomach, passing blood and pain. These are the same symptoms that I had when I was a child, between the ages of nine and thirteen. At that time, I was diagnosed as having peptic ulcers, a diagnosis that was confirmed by X-rays. On the basis of my current symptoms, my physician prescribed a diet and pills and referred me to the hospital insisting that I have X-rays before returning to him. The hospital's Neurology clinic referred me here. My symptoms occur after eating and particularly after drinking. Although I know I should not drink, alcohol helps me with some problems that have developed since my marriage four years ago, such as tension and sleeplessness. For these purposes, alcohol works better for me than pills that have been prescribed.

Some of the elements in her story emerge in response to the physician's questions; others appear without being directly elicited. All of the connections among the separate elements that allow us to recover a coherent narrative from fragments that appear in a different order in the interview are provided by the patient. Some of these connections are made explicitly, such as her linking of current to childhood symptoms. Thus, after affirming, in response to the physician's questions, that passing "blood clots" was one of her childhood symptoms, she goes on: "............ In fact this is last time too. .... That's why I came here because I- I- that's what ya know that's- my other one started that way" (062). Other links are more implicit, such as her specification of a particular triad of symptoms that she has currently and had as a child: pain, sour stomach, and passing blood. There is a similar implicit link between her statement of her own physician's insistence that she have X-rays now and her report that X-rays confirmed the diagnosis of peptic ulcers when she was a child.

In the first step of this reanalysis, I have been trying to bring the patient's story forward and give it a more prominent place in our understanding of the interview. To this end, I have presented a version of her story, reconstructed from the interview but using only elements and connections that she provides. I have also argued that an effort is required for such a reconstruction since the physician systematically interrupts her telling of the story. An example will show one way in which he does this.

At the end of the patient's first statement in which she describes why she was referred and her physician's recommendations (007-016), the physician says: "………. Okay now you've had . according to this thing ………….. uh:m …………… you haven- you had an ulcer at age *nine?*" (018). When referring to this statement earlier, I called it interruption by inattention. With the patient's full story in mind, we can now understand more fully how this comment functions as an interruption. First, we can see that, although her terms are vague, the patient has included in her statement many of the central elements of her story that will later be elaborated and specified. She refers to her current symptoms which we will learn are pain, sour stomach, and passing blood. She indicates her physician's stress on X-rays which we will find is connected to the use of X-rays to confirm the diagnosis of peptic ulcers when she was a child.

In earlier analyses, I treated the physician's "Hm Hm" (017), prior to completion of the patient's statement, and his "Okay" (018) as he begins his own question, as "assessments." That is, I viewed them as attention markers indicating that, at the least, the physician was showing that he heard the patient and was minimally acknowledging her statement. This is the usual interpretation of such brief insertion comments and turn-beginning items. However, in the specific context of the patient's account, although "Okay" serves to introduce the physician's next question, it appears to serve an interrupting function as well. In particular, the full phrase, "Okay now," closes off the patient's statement from what follows. Metaphorically speaking, the comment is a "bridge" for the physician linking the cycles of turn-taking through which he attempts to maintain control of the interview, but it is also a "barrier" to the patient since it prevents her from taking the floor and continuing with her story. "Okay" followed by "now" means "enough of that." Thus, this is an active interruption of the patient's story, rather than an invitation to continue.

I noted earlier that the physician's question began with reference to a document, presumably the patient's chart, rather than with her statement, and that the content of his question had no prior point of reference to her talk. Now, we can see more clearly what is ignored. Despite the patient's vagueness, the physician does not ask her to clarify her statement. He does not, for example, ask: "What symptoms are you having?", "Why did your physician put you on a diet, and what pills did he give you?", "Why was he so insistent on your having X-rays?" Since he does not ask her to make more sense of these information fragments the patient will have to find other ways than responses to his questions to make her account more coherent and sensible.

From these preliminary observations directed towards a recentering of the interview around the patient's story, I want to turn to a more systematic description and analysis of the voices of the lifeworld and medicine and of the dialectic between them.

The Voices of the Lifeworld and of Medicine: Dialectics of the Interview

The concept of voices was introduced in Chapter 3 and given a preliminary definition as the realization in speech of underlying normative orders. As used in those analyses, it referred to the overall tenor and thrust of medical interviews. In particular, the voice of medicine functioned analytically as a relatively abstract and summary characterization of the variety of ways in which physicians were shown to control the organization and content of interviews. The voice of the lifeworld was less well-defined and tended to refer to statements by patients that departed from the "normative" voice of medicine, occasionally disrupting the fluent flow of an interview.

In this section, the concept of voices will be developed and applied in a more systematic way and will be given primary attention in the analysis. As I shall be using the term, a voice represents a structure of meanings; these structures will be ascertained through examination of the ways of speaking. Both physician and patient may speak in either voice and each may switch voices within or between utterances or turns. Furthermore, the discourse is shaped by the ways the voices interrupt and interpenetrate each other. These considerations are fundamental to the following analyses.

The particular contents that define and differentiate the voices from each other will be specified more clearly as the analysis proceeds. As a preliminary gloss, the voice of the lifeworld refers to the patient's contextually-grounded experiences of events and problems in her life. These are reports and descriptions of the world of everyday life expressed from the perspective of a "natural attitude."[4] The timing of events and their significance are dependent on the patient's biographical situation and position in the social world. In contrast, the voice of medicine reflects a "technical" interest and expresses a "scientific attitude." The meaning of events is provided through abstract rules that serve to decontextualize events, to remove them from particular personal and social contexts. These definitions will be used as heuristics for the initial and tentative step of distinguishing between and classifying stretches of the interview as representing one or the other voice.

In order to discern more clearly how the two "voices" differ from each other and how together they produce discourse, new transcribing rules are necessary. This might seem strange and trivial, but I have already pointed out that transcripts are not neutral descriptions of talk, but incorporate models of language. The transcripts used for analysis in the previous chapter were constructed in terms of a view of discourse in which certain features of utterances and turn-taking were considered significant, such as length and location of silences, as well as overlaps between speakers.

The concept of the speaker's "slot" or "turn" was basic to much of the work I drew upon in conversation analysis, but it remains unexamined. When a "turn" is the central term in analysis, turn-taking, rather than topic-switching, is treated as the central problem (Sacks, Schegloff, & Jefferson, 1974) and a speaker's uninterrupted statement is simply an undifferentiated piece of talk; it is the space that is filled between the turns of

---

[4] The distinction between "natural" and "scientific" attitudes may be found in Schutz (1962); see particularly, Part I, "Commonsense and scientific interpretations of human action," and Part III, "On multiple realities."

other speakers. Further, since a "conversation" is also viewed as a unitary event, separate "conversations" within the flow of discourse have to be treated as distractions, as side sequences, or as embedded sequences whose removal does not radically alter the structure and flow of the "conversation" (Jefferson, 1972; Schegloff, Jefferson, & Sacks, 1977). The idea of separate voices and of their interpenetration in the production of conversation suggests that a different way of organizing and arranging the transcript may reveal these voices at work.

I have suggested that description is a first level of analysis and that transcriptions of interviews incorporate and represent models of languages that also enter into further analyses. In developing new transcription rules, I wish to include features of discourse that I have been proposing as significant to our understanding of how the voices of the lifeworld and of medicine interact to shape and organize the developing form and content of the interview. The modified rules are intended to differentiate the two voices in a stronger and clearer way than the rules used earlier; first, by using two different type faces, one for each voice; and second, by treating shifts between voices as interruptions, whether they occur within or between speaker turns.

Figure 4.1 compares two transcripts of the same brief section of an interview. The first example is taken from transcript 3.3 in Chapter 3 (W:13.121/01); the second transcription follows the new rules. The interruption of one voice by another is marked within the text by a "[" as interruptions had been marked earlier. However, in the new model, speakers may interrupt themselves as they switch from one voice to another. Interruptions are also marked in the margin lines that frame cycles of voices within the interview; these breaks are indicated by "w." Notations in the margin also indicate whether the stretch of talk is in the voice of medicine, "M1 ...", or the voice of the lifeword, "L1 ..."

The structural unit of discourse that was interpreted earlier as the essential feature of medical interviews is shown clearly in the first transcript as V. It begins with the physician's question, "How- How soon after you eat it?" It is followed by the patient's response which is interrupted by a clarification question, and is terminated with the physician's question which begins the next unit, ".......... Does drinking make it worse?" The alternative possibility that this stretch of talk might be divided into two units

Figure 4.1 Comparison of Transcripts Based on Different Models of Discourse

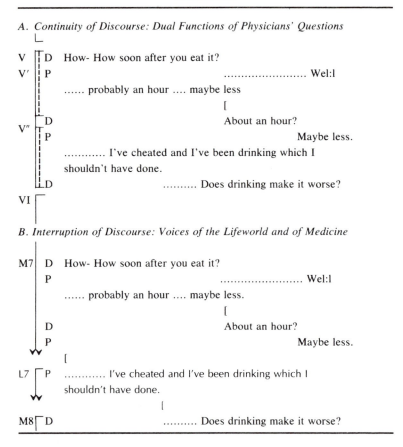

A. Continuity of Discourse: Dual Functions of Physicians' Questions

V   D How- How soon after you eat it?
V' P   .... Wel:l
       ...... probably an hour .... maybe less
                                        [
    D   About an hour?
V" P   Maybe less.
       .... I've cheated and I've been drinking which I
       shouldn't have done.
    D   .... Does drinking make it worse?
VI

B. Interruption of Discourse: Voices of the Lifeworld and of Medicine

M7 D How- How soon after you eat it?
    P   .... Wel:l
       ...... probably an hour .... maybe less.
                                        [
    D   About an hour?
    P   Maybe less.
       [
L7 P .... I've cheated and I've been drinking which I
       shouldn't have done.
                         [
M8 D   .... Does drinking make it worse?

is indicated in the Chart by dashed lines and the alternate unit numbering of V' and V".

The retranscription of these exchanges gives us a different picture of discourse; one that is related to a different interpretation of what is going on between patient and physician. The different appearance of the transcript represents the different meaning assigned in the interruption analysis to the shift within the patient's turn from the voice of medicine to the voice of the lifeworld. This shift takes place after her direct answer (''Maybe less'') to his specification question, "About an hour?" After a pause, she goes on: "I've cheated and I've been drinking which I shouldn't have done." This second part of her utterance is in the voice of the lifeworld. In this exchange, the physician does not follow the patient's lead, but returns immediately to the voice of medicine with his next question: "Does drinking make it worse?" His question constitutes and is marked as another interruption in this reanalysis, although it was not viewed in this light in the earlier one.

The transcript of a longer excerpt from this interview, constructed according to the new rules, appears in an appendix to this chapter. It reveals a very different type of discourse than was apparent in the transcripts presented earlier. Rather than a series of connected cycles that gave a sense of a coherent and continuous interview organized and regulated by how questions and responses function as part of a turn-taking system, we now have an interview that appears to be fragmented. An important assumption of this new analysis is that our impression of fragmentation is not simply an artifact of how the transcript is arranged, but the transcript as a display represents a reconceptualization of the discourse of medical interviews. In other words, the transcribing rules and the resulting transcript are tools for representing more adequately a new conception of the medical interview as discourse between different voices.

A closer examination of those points in the discourse where there is a shift between voices may make more precise our general sense of fragmentation. These shifts are marked in the transcript: the lifeworld cycles are noted as L1, L2, ... Ln; those in the voice of medicine as M1, M2, ... Mn. Of the 10 instances where there is a switch from the lifeworld to medical voice (all of these done by the physician), three take place within the same utterance or speaker turn. All three of these have the same form; a brief assessment comment followed by a question on either a new topic or on a medically relevant point in her response: "Okay" (018), or "Hm hm" (066 and 130). In all three instances, the content of the lifeworld segment is essentially ignored. The physician's attention is selective even when he refers directly to an item in her account. Thus in L6, she talks about her diet that she doesn't "dare go off" because she will get a "sour stomach." The physician focuses on the symptom: ".... Now what do you mean by a sour stomach?" (131).

The implication of this abrupt shift in voice by the physician is that the content expressed in the voice of the lifeworld could be removed from the discourse without breaking the coherence or continuity that represents the voice of medicine. In other words, the apparent coherence of the interview found in earlier analyses is achieved by excluding the content of the lifeworld. This discontinuity is true of all but 3 of the 10 changes in voice made by the physician. In two of the latter, the physician's question is a request for clarification (028 and 095). In only one instance, after the patient's introduction of drinking as a problem (153), does the physician's next question refer directly to the content introduced by the patient: "......... Does drinking make it worse?" (156). Even in this instance as in the earlier question about the meaning of a sour stomach, he ignores that part of her statement where she refers to having "cheated." Thus, the general impression of fragmentation is a valid reflection of marked shifts in content as the physician cuts off the voice of the lifeworld and re-enters the discourse in the voice of medicine.

Of the 10 shifts from the voice of medicine to the voice of the lifeworld, 9 are done by the patient. In contrast to how the physician makes transitions between voices, all of those by the patient are within utterances. In all but one of these, the patient first answers the physician's question and then adds other content. In earlier analyses I referred to this new material as "surplus" content and noted that it was usually introduced in the form of tag comments. In the revised model of the interview developed here, these utterances, with their internal shifts in voices, are viewed as efforts by the patient to maintain coherence and continuity in her account. She first acknowledges the physician's prior question, in a more adequate way than the attention markers he displays in response to her statements, before adding further content. In four of the eight within-utterance transitions, the patient also marks the shift by a long pause or by a change in tone between her answer and the new content. For example, in the shift from M4 to L4, the patient first answers the physician's question about whether she had blood clots with her first or second ulcer and then adds other information about the relevance of these symptoms to her current situation. "Both .... In fact this is last time too .... That's why I came here because I- [D: Hm hm] I-that's what ya know that's- my other one started that way" (061).

The physician, on the other hand, makes little effort to maintain continuity with the patient's world of meanings. For example, in the physician's utterances, lifeworld segments are almost totally lacking in content. They consist almost entirely of the minimal acknowledgement, "Hm hm." Of the 10 comments made by the physician through all of the lifeworld segments, 7 are "Hm hm" and 1 is an "Okay." One is a clarification question which repeats the patient's words and therefore does not add content, "The first one?" (025). One is the response that is the physician's sole initiation of a lifeworld segment, "-and what happened in January?" (089).

The picture is quite different in the medical voice segments; of the physician's 44 utterances only 6 are limited to "Hm hm." Explicit token acknowledgements of this kind, even as part of a fuller utterance, are often lacking in the medical voice segments. Instead, acknowledgement often takes the form of repeating the patient's response as in (052) "No:o," or (082) "it went away." In some instances, there is a request for clarification or specification indicating that the patient's statement has been heard, for example, (056) "Bright red?" or (059) "With the first one or the second one?"

The structure of the interview is shown schematically in the form of a flow diagram in Figure 4.2. An example from the interview is presented in Figure 4.3 in terms of this schematic model. It includes the section of transcript from 059-073. This begins with the physician's question about blood clots with her ulcers: "........ With the first one or the second one?" The patient answers and then in the same utterance, preceded by a pause, she introduces a new topic in the voice of the lifeworld; this is followed by the physician's "Hm hm." She then elaborates on the topic. Again, her comment is followed by the physician's "Hm hm," but in the same utterance he switches back to the voice of medicine with a new question. The patient answers and then again presents new information. This time there is no attention marker by the physician; he immediately returns with a new question in the voice of medicine.

This schematic representation of the interview helps to clarify and highlight some of the points made earlier about the fragmentation of the discourse, the ways in which the voice of medicine interrupts the voice of the lifeworld, how the patient attempts to

Figure 4.2 Flow-Diagram Model of Sequencing Rules for Discourse Between the Voice of the Lifeworld and the Voice of Medicine

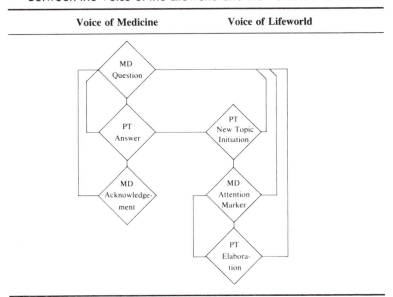

maintain coherence both in her account and over the disruptions of it by the physician, and the ways in which control is exercised by the physician. One implication of this structure stands out: there are many different routes back to a physician's question. Every utterance, by either physician or patient, and in either voice, can be followed by a question from the physician. It is a dense network of pathways, all of which return to the same point of origin.

I have already pointed to the powerful role that questions play in controlling the turn-taking system and the structure of the discourse in terms of speaker sequences, utterance lengths, and utterance types. These are relatively formal features of the language of discourse. Now, we can see that the flow of content toward the lifeworld or toward medicine is also controlled by the same conversational device, a question by the physician. In this new analysis, however, two additional characteristics become evident. First, it is not only that the physician asks questions, but that these questions are almost always in the voice of medicine and therefore serve to move the discourse away from topics of the lifeworld introduced by the patient. Second, these questions do

Figure 4.3 Flow Diagram Model: Interview Example

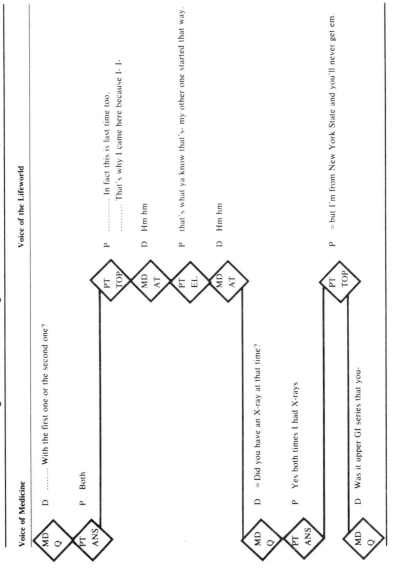

Voice of Medicine

MD Q   D   .... With the first one or the second one?

PT ANS   P   Both

MD Q   D   = Did you have an X-ray at that time?

PT ANS   P   Yes both times I had X-rays

MD Q   D   Was it upper GI series that you-

Voice of the Lifeworld

PT TOP   P   .... In fact this is last time too.
                         .... That's why I came here because 1- 1-

MD AT   D   Hm hm

PT EL   P   that's what ya know that's- my other one started that way.

MD AT   D   Hm hm

PT TOP   P   = but I'm from New York State and you'll never get em.

more than regulate the sequential organization of the interview through the turn-taking system; they also function as points of return from any other utterance. All roads lead back to the physician's question. In contrast, lifeworld topics introduced by the patient lead only to self-elaboration of the topic, at best; the discourse is then returned to point zero by the physician's question in the voice of medicine.

How the Voices Mean: The Structuring of Content

Up to now, my analysis has focused on how interaction between the two voices shapes and structures discourse. Shifts within responses by the patient from the voice of medicine to the voice of the lifeworld and shifts by the physician in the reverse direction received particular attention. The apparent coherence and orderliness of the interview found in earlier analyses was contrasted with the fragmentation uncovered in these new analyses. It seemed clear, as well, that different meanings were being expressed in the two voices. This difference was the implicit basis for distinguishing between stretches of talk as representing one or another voice. However, particular meanings and their organization have not yet been explicated. This section is directed to this problem; it is an exercise in the analysis of meaning.

Figure 4.4 is an abstract and schematized version of all but two of the physician's questions. From the top to the bottom of the figure, the sequential ordering of his questions is retained. With the exception of "and what happened in January?" (089), and "Now what do you mean by a sour stomach?" (131), his questions are all variants of a general stem focusing on whether the patient "had" a particular sign or experience, or "did" something specific. The general form is: "Did/do you have/do—?" or "Were/are you having/doing—?"

After his opening comment/question about her referral source, the physician's questions are directed at locating "when" the patient's different symptoms appeared. Although the three time periods to which he refers—childhood, since childhood, and the present—are sequentially ordered, his questions treat them separately from each other rather than as developmentally linked together. They are simply different periods only related to each other in a chronological sense. Within each period and topic, his ques-

Figure 4.4   Physician's Questions: Structure of the Voice of Medicine

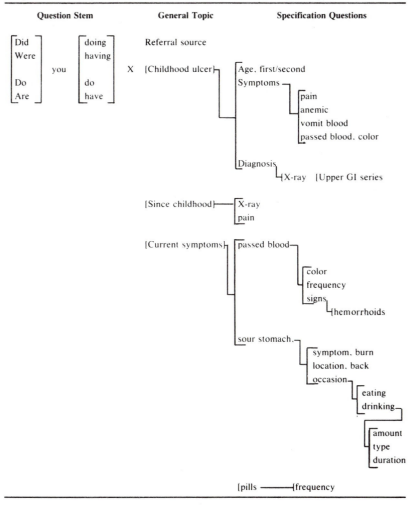

tions move from the general to the specific. The type of specification in this movement is of particular significance. It is directed toward a description of the patient's symptoms in objective physical terms. Thus, with reference to the symptom of "passing blood," the physician asks about its color, the frequency of occurrence, and the concrete signs through which the symptom is evident. With reference to the patient's report of a sour stomach, he asks about the sensation experienced, body location, occasions of occurrence, the temporal relation to eating, and the amount, type, and duration of her drinking.

There is another tendency towards objectification of reference in the movement of questions, although it is not uniform throughout the question sequences in the interview. This is the tendency for general questions to be framed with the second person subject, for example, "…. Now what do you mean by a sour stomach?" (131), with the follow-up questions phrased in terms of impersonal subjects, "Does it burn over here?" (134), and "Hm hm does it go into the back?" (141).

From these observations, a preliminary characterization of the structure of meaning represented in the voice of medicine would include the following: primary emphasis is given to the description of reality in terms of its objective, physical features. The questions include: What does it look/feel like? Where is it? When does it happen? How often does it happen? How much of it do you do/have? What makes it better/worse? Of course, such questions might also result in "subjective" answers in another context. But in the medical interview, an appropriate answer is one that refers to objective physical signs or indicators of the problem. If an answer is not objective in these terms, the physician will ask the question again. Thus, to the physician's question "How long have you been drinking that heavily?" (174), the patient responds, after a pause, "Since I've been married." The inadequacy and perhaps inappropriateness, from the physician's biomedical perspective, of this response is made clear by the physician who immediately restates his question, "How long is that?"

The primary emphasis on an "objective" reality that has standardized physical properties for all persons is also an exclusive one. I noted earlier the absence of reference to other content presented by the patient and proposed this as a principal source of the discontinuities in discourse between the voice of medicine and the lifeworld. This is strongly confirmed in Figure 4.4. None of these questions refer to any content other than the physical/objective features of the patient's report of symptoms.

Another quality of this structure is the lack of connection among its parts. Although each general topic is pursued through some level of specific detail, no connections are made across topics. For example, the time periods are not related to each other in any coherent way, nor are the different symptoms of pain, passing blood, and sour stomach linked together through the pattern of questioning. The various contents are discrete and separated from each other. This adds to the impression of fragmentation in the interview.

Despite the lack of connection in the surface content of the physician's questions about different topics, we could assume that they express a particular model of causality. From our general understanding of medical practice, it would seem likely to the patient, and to us as observers, that the physician is working with an underlying conceptual framework that specifies relationships among discrete and separate symptoms. However, there is no evidence of this model in the discourse and it would be understandable if the patient is confused by shifts in the content of the physician's questions and has no clear idea of what he is trying to discover.

Examination of the patient's speech in the voice of the lifeworld reveals a very different structure of meaning. Figure 4.5 outlines the patient's utterances in each of the lifeworld episodes. It is striking to find that all of them are variants of the same basic structure, although the sequential ordering of its components varies. The eight component terms are shown in their general form at the top of the figure. They are: (a) an optional Tie-marker that links together components of the patient's story; (b) the acting subject (the patient in all but two cases), in which the first person reference is retained through the possessive "my"; (c) an action or state of the subject which is the predicate term in the clause; (d) a conjunction linking the first part to the second part of the utterance, almost always the explicit causal term "because," or causality implied by ellipsis; (e) the acting subject; (f) a second action or state of the subject; (g) the symptom or problem that is the reason for the subject's action in the first half of the utterance; and (h) the time in the patient's life when the symptom or problem occurred.

Another, more formal way to describe this structure is that it consists of a first part made up of an intransitive verb clause connected through a causal conjunction to a second verb clause that is usually also intransitive. An optional Tie-marker may initiate the first clause; an optional time reference may terminate the second clause.

Figure 4.5 Patient's Statements: Structure of the Lifeworld*

	Tie-Marker	Subject	Predicate	Conjunction	Subject	Predicate	Object	Time
L1	First	My doctor	put me on diet / gave me pills / told me X-rays	(because of my symptoms)				
L2					I	had	first ulcer / second one	age 9 / 2 years later
L3		My doctor	shocked to death	because	he	never knew	2 ulcers	girl my age
L4		I	came here	That's why	other this one	started	this way too	
L5	Finally	I	couldn't stand it anymore	(because I)	kept getting	sour stomach passed blood	week, two before	
L6	Now	I	on diet don't dare go off	because	I	end up with	sour stomach	

L7	(I)		(because)	[I]	[cheated / drinking / shouldn't have done]	(sour stomach)
L8	[I've]	(drink) enough	[to]		[get]	[to sleep]
L9	[I've]	(drinking heavily)	since	[I've]	[been married]	
L10	[I]	[drinking beer]	(because I)		[had a job / more things on mind]	[before marriage]
	[I]	[(need) somethin to go to sleep]	(because I)		[been in and outa jobs]	[since marriage]
	[I]	[(prefer) alcohol to pills]	(because)	[alcohol / pills]	[satisfies me / not strong enough]	

* Words in brackets [ ] are the patient's own words in summary form; words in parentheses ( ) refer to what is implied by ellipsis in a statement.

The most complete patient utterance that represents the full structure and requires little "redoing" or rearranging is diagrammed as L6 (127–129) in the typescript:

> "I'm on a diet now and I don't dare go off it because if I do I end up with a sour stomach."

Others are almost as complete, with perhaps an ellipsis for the causal connection and an inversion of the two clauses as in L5 (090–093):

> "I kept getting a sour stomach a:n went on for at least two weeks and finally I couldn't stand it anymore and I passed blood about .. a week or two before"

This has been reorganized in the figure in the following way:

> [Finally] [I] [couldn't stand it anymore] (because) [I] [kept getting]
> [a sour stomach] & [passed blood] [a week or two before]

A second similar full statement is L10 (183-185); this is also inverted in the figure, but the basic structure is apparent after reorganization:

> "but since I got married I been in and out of jobs and everything so .... I- I have ta have somethin to go to sleep."
> [ ] [I] [have ta have somethin to go to sleep] (because) [I] [been]
> [in and out of jobs and everything] [since I got married]

Abstracting utterances from the actual discourse and reorganizing them in terms of formal categories of speech is a risky procedure, particularly if our task is to determine the structure of meaning as it is revealed in talk. This procedure has been adopted, for both physician and patient utterances, in order to show more clearly the features of the different deep structures of meaning that take variant surface forms.

What meanings are expressed in the voice of the lifeworld, and how do they contrast with those in the voice of medicine? First, there is the causally contingent nature of events in the patient's world of experience. Her doctor is "shocked to death" "because" she had two ulcers when she was a young child; she doesn't "dare

go off' her diet "because" she'll "end up with a sour stomach";
she drinks alcohol because of problems of tension and sleeplessness developing since her marriage; and she drinks rather than
takes pills because the former works better for her. She has come
for medical treatment and X-rays at this time because her current
symptoms are similar to those she had as a child.

It is clear from her way of talking that events in her world are
connected in a causally meaningful way. Further, these events
are self-centered; these are her symptoms, her pains, her marriage,
her sleeplessness, and her drinking. There is a coherence to her
account that is provided, in part, by the repetition of certain actions or states, for example, her drinking and sour stomach. In
addition, there is the linking of past and present through the similarity of symptoms; passing blood is related to the fact that her
"other one started that way." Finally, events are temporally ordered relative to each other; she passed blood "a week or two
before" she began getting a sour stomach and she's been drinking
heavily since her marriage, but had "more things" on her mind
before marriage.

This coherence of meanings, revealed in the structure of her
utterances only after their reorganization, is obscured in the discourse because the flow and organization of her narrative account
is disrupted by the physician. The presentation of an account that
is coherent and meaningful in the patient's terms requires active
work on her part because she is interrupted throughout its course
by the physician speaking in the voice of medicine. I have made
this point before, but now it is possible to define more precisely
how this happens. The structure of the physician's questions,
outlined in Figure 4.4, is based on a series of linked specification
questions, each a separate subseries focused on a particular
symptom. This logical structure is very different from that of the
patient's. The physician's questions are directed towards the definition and classification of each item in turn, rather than towards
relations among items.

Further, relations among symptoms that might be inferred from
his questions have nothing to do with the causal relations among
life events reported by the patient. It is particularly instructive to
discover that none of the physician's questions refer to the first-
part clauses or the causal connections in the patient's utterances.
Instead they are directed only to the symptom included in the
second clause. For example, after the patient's full statement in

L6 (127–129), "I'm on a diet now and I don't dare go off it because if I do I end up with a sour stomach," the physician responds with "Hm hm .... Now what do you mean by a sour stomach?" After her complex account about her need and reasons for using alcohol rather than pills to help her get to sleep and "quiet me down during the day" (L10), the physician responds with "…. How often do you take them?"

The net effect of the physician's interruptions are to strip away the contexts of the patient's experience of her problem. He ignores the causally structured and temporarily-ordered connections that she describes. He focuses on one element in her account, the "objective" symptom, removes it from the grounding she gives it in her life, and isolates each element from the others.

I noted earlier that as members of this culture we, as observers, and the patient, are likely to assume that the physician has "reasons" for his questions. It is somewhat remarkable, but understandable on the basis of this shared assumption, that the patient does not reject any of his questions as inappropriate, however disjunctive they are with previous content, but makes an effort to answer them.[5] Presumably the physician's questions reflect the biomedical model with its specification of the significance of symptoms and their relations to each other as indicators of particular disease processes. The standard form of a diagnostic examination that he is following, as in the unremarkable interviews examined earlier, is one of the principal ways in which this model has been transformed into practice. Nonetheless, the model is not made explicit to the patient. It is invisible and inaudible in the discourse.

The above interpretation of different structures of meaning represented in the voices of the lifeworld and of medicine is based directly on what is audible/visible in the discourse. The analyses have led to a markedly different view of the medical interview than that presented earlier. Rather than displaying continuity through the physician's control of turn-taking and the dual func-

---

[5] I have occasionally asked medical students if there are any questions that might be inappropriate to ask at any point in a medical examination. They are puzzled by this query and usually come up with only very bizarre possibilities. Patients appear to accept this broad and open-ended view of what they can be asked and they respond to any and all questions as legitimate and appropriate, even when they do not seem to understand their purpose.

tions of his questions, the discourse has been shown to be marked by discontinuities, by disruptions of the patient's account, and by a pattern of questioning that functions to strip away lifeworld contexts of meaning. By interrupting my earlier analysis and placing the patient's account at the center of inquiry, a different understanding of the nature of unremarkable interviews and standard clinical practice emerged. The discourse of medical interviews is not to be understood primarily as one dominated by physicians speaking in the voice of medicine with patients intruding their concerns, thereby disrupting its smooth flow. Rather, discourse is revealed as a dialectic between the voices of the lifeworld and of medicine; it involves conflict and struggle between two different domains of meaning.

Provinces of Meaning and Modes of Consciousness: Voices In Context

Social theory is not a strong feature in studies of medical interviews. Reports tend to be limited to presentations of empirical findings or to narrowly-focused interpretations that neither place such interviews in broader contexts of social practices nor relate them to more general theoretical issues. Thus, typical studies such as those reviewed in Chapter 2 may focus on the relative rates of positive and negative affect in physician and patient statements (Korsh & Negrete, 1972) or on the proportion of physician statements containing information. (Waitzkin et al., 1978; Waitzkin & Stoeckle, 1976). The significance of certain persistent findings is left unexplored. For example, although difficulties in communication and misunderstandings between patients and physicians are found in study after study, these problems, with rare exceptions,[6] are not examined from the perspective of a general social theory.

The interpretation of the medical interview as a dialectic between the voices of the lifeworld and of medicine is a first step in the direction of a more general perspective. In this concluding section, I wish to extend and develop this interpretation by drawing upon two strong traditions in social theory: phenomenological

---

[6] For an exception to this generalization about the lack of social theory, see Waterman and Waitzkin (1977); see Hauser (1981) for a review of more typical studies.

sociology and critical theory. In particular, I will apply Shutz' concept of provinces of meaning and Habermas' distinction between symbolic and rational-purposive interaction.

Schutz (1962) describes several provinces of meaning, each characterized by a particular attitude toward the world. The "natural attitude" or "attitude of everyday life" is the mode of consciousness within which we act in our daily lives. It is the ordinary "common sense" world of social reality. The hallmark of this attitude is a suspension of doubt; the way the world appears to be is accepted as what it is. The self is the center of space and time coordinates in the sense that events are located and given significance with reference to one's own biographical situation and location in the world. In the natural attitude, events take on relevance from their relationship to the acting subject's interests, purposes, and plans. Motives are pragmatic; the primary meaning of events is in how they may affect the achievement of purposes and in how one's actions may change the world. A logic of use and a criterion of reasonableness provide the basis on which one makes sense of events and actions in the world.

Schutz compares a number of other attitudes with the natural attitude. His analysis of the "scientific" attitude is particularly relevant to this discussion. The perspective of a person in the scientific attitude is that of a "disinterested" observer. Events in the world are not viewed within subjective coordinates of space and time, but with reference to abstract, standard, and context-free coordinates of "objective" space and time. Events and actions receive their meaning from their location in a general scheme or model from which pragmatic motives have been removed. Interest in the world is theoretical. The criteria of scientific rationality and formal logic provide the grounds for assessing the meaning and significance of events.

Even from this brief sketch of Schutz' concepts, it is evident that there is a fairly close congruence between attitudes and their corresponding provinces of meaning and the concept of voices that represent structures of meaning. This concept has emerged from and is used in my analyses of medical interviews. Respectively, the voices of the lifeworld and of medicine appear to be direct counterparts of natural and scientific attitudes. Tentatively, the two voices might be thought of as the ways in which these contrasting attitudes and their associated meanings are expressed in discourse, within the special and particular context of the medical interview.

Schutz proposes that the natural attitude and the common sense world are basic social "realities," and that all other attitudes are "modifications." That is, the scientific attitude refers to a second-order construction of the common sense world. He makes the further point that since different attitudes represent different provinces of meaning, each with its own logic and structure, that they cannot be transformed directly into each other, nor can one be reduced to the other without serious distortion.

Schutz does not discuss the question of central concern in these analyses; what happens when two attitudes or voices enter into the same discourse. From his formulation, we would expect to find evidence of disruption, problems in maintaining coherence, and misunderstandings. And indeed, a variety of these problems appear and have been explicated in earlier sections of this chapter. The medical interview may be viewed as an arena of struggle between the natural attitude with its common sense lifeworld and the scientific attitude with its objectified world of abstract logic and rationality.

Nonetheless, the situation I have been describing is an interview in which patient and physician continue to talk to each other despite their difficulties. Thus, there are ways in which a discourse between two different voices can be sustained. This is not accomplished by both parties fully adopting one of the two voices; the physician does not shift to the voice of the lifeworld nor does the patient speak only in the voice of medicine. Nor is the interview sustained through translation of one voice into the other by either speaker. Schutz implies that such a translation, a transformation of one province of meaning into another, would not be possible; at a minimum, we would expect that a great deal would be lost in the effort. Nor have we seen the development of a full dialogue between the two voices where, if not a true reciprocity of perspectives, some attempt is made to take the perspective of the other into account.

Rather, continuity of discourse appears to have been maintained through two conversational strategies. One is the process of selective attention on the physician's part. He responds to one element of the patient's account, usually her mention of a specific symptom, abstracts it from the context within which it is presented, and then refers to the symptom within another context expressed in the voice of medicine. The symptom is thus transformed by being relocated to a different province of meaning. As we have seen, much is lost in the translation from one voice to another. It is as if a poem in one language that uses qualities of the weather, such as its dampness or coldness, as a metaphor for the feeling state of the narrator were to be translated literally into another language as a description of the weather.

The patient's efforts to maintain continuity are of a different sort. She tries to stay in touch with the voice of medicine by connecting her statements in response to the physician's questions. At the same time, she adds other information, often in the voice of the lifeword. Thus, she attempts to retain her meaning of her problem in its experienced context and, thereby, keep her own perspective alive in the discourse.

Schutz states that the reciprocity of perspectives that informs the natural attitude and permits us to coordinate our actions with others in the shared, intersubjective common sense world is dependent upon and sustained through face-to-face interaction. Although two persons are talking to each other in the medical interview, it does not have the essential reciprocity feature of ordinary face-to-face interaction and might more precisely be viewed as face-to-mask interaction.

Schutz' conception of provinces of meaning is useful as a way to understand some of the more general characteristics of the separate voices in the interview. However, he does not directly address situations of interaction. Habermas' (1970)[7] distinction between symbolic and rational-purposive interaction relates somewhat more closely to our problem. His two terms have zones of reference that overlap with and are consistent with Schutz' natural and scientific attitudes, and his criteria for distinguishing between these two types of interaction are quite similar to Schutz' description of these contrasting provinces of meaning.

Habermas states that symbolic interaction is oriented towards social norms. It reflects and depends upon an intersubjectively shared ordinary language and reciprocal expectations about behavior, and is sustained through conformity to mutually-agreed upon social norms. The realm of purposive-rational or instrumental interaction, sometimes referred to as the domain of work, has other features. It is oriented towards technical rules, aimed at efficiency of problem-solving through the application and extension of technical control, and uses a context-free language.

---

[7] For a fine and perceptive analysis of the problem posed by the power of the technocratic consciousness, discovered after completing this study, see Stanley (1978).

Habermas uses this distinction to develop a critique of the domination of the social world by technology or the triumph of the technocratic consciousness in the modern world. Although he is addressing large-scale sociopolitical issues, his comments apply to the situation of the medical interview. This is readily seen when we recognize that the voice of medicine is one version of the technocratic consciousness and that a physician's attempt to dominate the interview, by transforming a patient's lifeworld problems into technical-medical problems, is only one of the manifestations of a more general sociohistorical trend.

Habermas points to some of the problems and consequences of the domination of technological considerations:

> What seems to me more important is that it [the technocratic consciousness] can also become a background ideology that penetrates into the consciousness of the depoliticized mass of the population, where it can take on legitimating power. It is a singular achievement of this ideology to detach society's self-understanding from the frame of reference of communicative action and from the concepts of symbolic interaction and replace it with a scientific mode. Accordingly, the culturally defined self-understanding of a social lifeworld is replaced by the self-reification of men under categories of purposive-rational action and adaptive behavior. ... the structure of one of the two types of action, namely the behavioral system of purposive-rational action, not only predominates over the institutional framework but gradually absorbs communicative actions as such. ... the institutional framework of society - which previously was rooted in a different type of action - would now, in a fundamental reversal, be *absorbed* by the subsystems of purposive-rational action, which were embedded in it. ... the dissolution of the sphere of linguistically mediated interaction by the structure of purposive-rational action. ... is paralleled subjectively by the disappearance of the difference between purposive-rational action and interaction from the consciousness not only of the sciences of man, but of men themselves. The concealment of this difference proves the ideological power of the technocratic consciousness. (pp. 105-107)

I have quoted Habermas at some length since I believe that his theoretical analysis clarifies and extends our understanding of the significance of particular ways of talking in medical interviews that have emerged in these analyses. If we substitute his concepts of purposive-rational action and its associated technocratic consciousness for the voice of medicine and that of symbolic interaction for the voice of the lifeworld, then we can recognize a "fundamental reversal" taking place in the medical interview. The physician's effort to control the discourse has the effect of absorbing and dissolving the patient's self-understanding of her problems into a system of purposive-rational action, namely, the framework of technical medicine.

Habermas outlines further consequences of the domination of the lifeworld by the technocratic consciousness that also apply directly to medical interviews:

> Technocratic consciousness reflects not the sundering of an ethical situation but the repression of "ethics" as such as a category of life. ... The ideological nucleus of this consciousness is the *elimination of the distinction between the practical and the technical.* ... The new ideology consequently violates an interest grounded in one of the two fundamental conditions of our cultural existence; in language, or more precisely, in the form of socialization and individuation determined by communication in ordinary language. This interest extends to the maintenance of intersubjectivity of mutual understanding as well as to the creation of communication without dominance. Technocratic consciousness makes this practical interest disappear behind the interest in the expansion of our power of technical control. (pp. 112-113)

Further,

> Only the technocratic consciousness obscures the fact that this reconstruction [conversion of practical to technical problems] could be achieved at no less a cost than closing off the only dimension that is essential, because it is susceptible to humanization, *as* a structure of interactions mediated by ordinary language." (p. 117)

Habermas' analysis locates Schutz' "provinces of meaning" within an historical and political context. This analysis encompasses more and has more profound consequences than is captured by the neutral notion of different "attitudes" or by the descriptive labels used by various investigators such as "patient talk" and "doctor talk" (Byrne & Long, 1976; Shuy, 1976). When the patient says: "... and finally I couldn't stand it anymore and I passed blood about .. a week or two before .... but ya know it didn't dawn on me at the time" (091–094), and the physician proceeds to ask a series of questions about when, how much, what color, and what signs while ignoring her experienced distress of not being able to "stand it anymore," he is dissolving the meaning and significance of events in her lifeworld. He is engaged in the fundamental reversal that Habermas cautions us against: of absorbing the lifeworld, the essential and basic "province of meaning," into the technical subsystem of medicine. When the patient responds to the physician's question, "How long have you been drinking that heavily?" with "................... Since I've been married," which locates her problem within a coordinate of subjective time, and the physician presses her toward objective time, "........ How long is that?" he is reconstructing her practical interests into technical ones.

Based on this dicussion and the preceding analyses, I am proposing an interpretation of the medical interview as a situation of conflict between two ways of constructing meaning. Moreover, I am also proposing that the physician's effort to impose a technocratic consciousness, to dominate the voice of the lifeworld by the voice of medicine, seriously impairs and distorts essential requirements for mutual dialogue and human interaction. To the extent that clinical practice is realized through this type of discourse, the possibility of more humane treatment in medicine is severely limited. As Habermas argues, the transformation of practical into technical interests, and the reconstruction of the lifeworld into a technical system of purposive-rational action, closes off the dimension that is essential for humanization of interaction, "a structure of interactions mediated by ordinary language" (p. 117).

In this last section, I have placed a revised interpretation of clinical practice within the context of a more general social theory. The view of medical interviews as a dialectic between the voices of the lifeworld and of medicine and the description and analysis of discourse from the perspective of the patient has been linked to a more general conflict within society between two modes of consciousness; the technocratic expressed through a language of purposive-rational action, and the symbolic expressed through ordinary language. Habermas' distinction, which maps closely on to the distinction between the two voices, is more than descriptive. It is also evaluative in that he specifies separate domains of relevance as appropriate for the two modes of consciousness and develops an argument about the negative consequences that follow the triumph of the technocratic consciousness. He asserts that where human interests are involved, the absorption of ordinary language by technical language leads to the distortion and suppression of human values; it substitutes technical-rational considerations for normative ones.

Medicine, of course, is a technical domain based on the rationalities of science. Nonetheless, this is only a partial definition. The practice of medicine is itself not a theoretical, but an applied science (Mishler et al., 1981). Its focus and aims are tied not to the "disinterested" stance of the scientific investigator, but to the practical concerns of patient care and treatment. I am proposing that the dominance of the voice of medicine is an example of the "absorption" of ordinary language by the system of purposive-rational action. In analyses of medical interviews, undertaken from the patient's point of view, I have shown that this leads to an "objectification" of the patient, to a stripping away of the lifeworld contexts of patient problems. For this reason, I have concluded that such a form of discourse severely limits, if it does not exclude entirely, the possibility of humane medical practice. The latter depends on maintaining the primacy of the lifeworld as the "essential" grounds of human action.

By going beyond description and the neutral interpretation of empirical findings to Habermas' conceptualization and his evaluative stance, I have been trying to open up alternatives of thought and action that are potential within the medical interview and clinical practice.[8] In the next chapter, a medical interview is examined in which the physician appears to be more attentive to the voice of the lifeworld. Some of the potential avenues for developing a more humane clinical practice are suggested by the analysis of this interview.

---

[8] The view that both the sciences and the arts must provide alternative perspectives rather than restrict themselves to descriptions or representations of reality, has a long history in Marxist thought. George Lukacs' work on literature, John Berger's essays on art and art criticism, and Jurgen Habermas' conception of an emancipatory science are particularly cogent examples of this tradition.

Appendix to Chapter 4

W:13.121/01. Voices of the Lifeworld and of Medicine

M1 ⌜ 001 D   I'm Doctor Gerson.

    002 P   (...) I know (what it is).

    003 D   Oka:y ....

    004   Now let's see . you were .. referred here .. actually they sent

    005   you up here from medical clinic .... from the . screening

    006.   clinic clinic rather.

    007 P   Yea:h. Well I was sent up here from uh-

    008   from neurology really .... because I told them- I

    009   told them what my symptoms were .... and uh they said

    010   Okay ...... we'll get you up there.

                                                   [

L1 ⌜ 011 P   .... But first I

    012   I went to see my doctor he put me on a diet he gave me some

                                          [

    013 D   Hm hm

    014 P   pills ...... and he said while you're in there go. ....

    015   .... In other words *don't* come back to me .... until you've

    016   had X-rays taken. .... That's what he implied.

                       [

    017 D   Hm hm   ......

    018 D   .... Okay

                    [

M2 ⌜ 019 D   = now you've had . according to this thing ....

    020   .... uh:m .... you haven- you had an ulcer

    021   at age *nine*?

    022 P   Um about- between nine- nine and eleven

                                        [

L2 ⌜ 023 P   at age *nine*? Um about- between nine- nine and eleven = I had the

    024   first one.

    025 D   The first one?

    026 P   And then- uh then two years later I

    027   developed a second one.

                      [

M3 ⌜ 028 D   .... That was about . thirteen or so.

                                   [

    029 P   Uh:m

```
      030        between- between nine- nine and thirteen ........
      031 P                                                   The only thing-
                                                                    [
      032 D                                                        That's
      033        when you had your second one.
      034 P                                      Yes:s.
                                                   [
L3    035 P                                       The only thing I can remember
      036        is that my doctor was shocked to death because he never knew a
      037        girl my- my age that had . two ulcers.
      038 D                                          Hm hm
      039 P                                              (...)
                                                           [
M4    040 D                                              And how did-
      041        how did the ulcers present. What uh- what happened? ......
      042        Just pain or uh
      043 P              It's a- wel:l . ye:ah . pa- lot- lots and lots
      044        of pain sour stomach
      045 D                 Hm hm
      046 P                        and most of the time I could feel my
      047        food going down and then when it would hit . the end of the tube
      048        it would just . drop right into my stomach.
      049 D                                      Were you anemic at
      050        the time?
      051 P             ............ No:o.
      052 D                     No:o. Did you vomit up any blood?
      053 P     No I passed blood.
      054 D                   What color was it?
      055 P                                 It was red .. there were clots.
                                                              [
      056 D                                                  Bright
      057        red?
      058 P        Yes. There were blood clots.
      059 D                            ........ With the first one or
      060        the second one?
      061 P                Both.
                             [
L4    062 P              ............ In fact this is last time too.
      063        .......... That's why I came here because I- I- that's what
                                          [
      064 D                              Hm hm
```

065 P   ya know that's- my other one started that way.

066 D   Hm hm

                                                    [

M5 067 D   =Did you have

      068   an X-ray at that time?

      069 P   Yes both times I had X-rays

                                                    [

    070 P   = but I'm from

      071   New York State and you'll never get em.

                                        [

      072 D   Was it upper GI series

      073   that you-

                  [

      074 P   Ye:s.

      075 D   And they told you that the ulcer showed up on .

      076   the X-ray?

      077 P   Ri:ght.

      078 D   And then . have you had any . X-rays since then

      079   .... of your stomach?

                  [

      080 P   No because I (...)-   No because I never had . ya

      081   know . it went away. They were peptic ulcers.

                                      [

      082 D   It went away.   Uh uh . and uh

      083   you've had no pain since then .

      084 P   Not until-

                                [

      085 D   Until now.

      086 P   ...... Not until

      087   January.

    088 D   Okay

                    [

L5 089 D   = and what happened in January.

      090 P   Well I got- I kept

      091   getting a sour stomach a:n went on for at least two weeks and

      092   finally I couldn't stand it anymore and I passed blood about ..

      093   a week or two before .... but ya know it didn't dawn on me at

      094   the time .... and uh-

                                      [

M6 095 D   What do you mean you say you

      096   passed blood a week or two before.

097 P   Wel:l it was sometime in

098   November or December that I had passed blood. .... But

099   my stomach didn't hurt then .... and then (...)-

                                                                       [

100 D   Was it

101   bright red blood that you passed?

                                      [

102 P   Yea:h

103 D   How many times did you pass it?

104 P   Oh jeez I don't remember.

105 D   .... Uh uh

106 P   I th- I can't tell ya

107   because I only saw . just the once.

108 D   I see. Was it on the toilet

109   paper or in the bowl?

                          [

110 P   No. It was in the bowl. It was in the um-

                                         [

111 D   It was in the

112   bowl. I see. .... Do you oft- do you ever get blood on the

113   toilet paper when you-

                      [

114 P   No. no.

115 D   Have you ever been told of hemorrhoids?

116 P   Oh yeah yeah. I've (...)-

                          [

117 P   I've had some friends that had

118   hemorrhoids but I've never had em.

                                          |

119 D   You've *never* had hemorrhoids?

120 P   No.

121 D   Never been told that (...) hm hm .... and then

122   you developed- starting in January you developed a sour *stom*ach.

123 P   Yes extremely.

124 D   For about two weeks. ...... And have you had

125   anything since then?

126 P   I've had a sour stomach.

                                                [

L6   127 P   I'm on a diet now

128   and I don't dare go off it because if I do I end up with a sour

129   stomach.

	130 D	Hm hm
		[
M7	131 D	.... Now what do you mean by a sour stomach?
	132 P	.... What's a sour stomach? A heartburn like a
	133	heartburn or something.
		[
	134 D	Does it burn over here?
	135 P	Yea:h. It li- I think-
	136	I think it like- If you take a needle and stick ya right ....
		[[
	137 D	Hm hm Hm hm
	138 P	there's a pain right here .. and then it goes from here on this
		[
	139 D	Hm hm
	140 P	= side to this side.
	141 D	Hm hm Does it go into the back?
		[
	142 P	It's a:ll up here. No. It's
	143	all right up here in front.
		[
	144 D	Yeah. And when do you get that?
	145 P	......
	146	.... Wel:l when I eat something wrong.
	147 D	How- How soon
	148	after you eat it?
	149 P	.... Wel:l ...... probably
	150	an hour .... maybe less.
		[
	151 D	About an hour?
	152 P	Maybe less.
		[
L7	153 P	.... I've
	154	cheated and I've been drinking which I shouldn't have done.
		[
M8	155 D	....
	156	...... Does drinking make it worse?
		[
	157 P	(...) Ho ho uh ooh Yes. ....
	158	Especially the carbonation and the alcohol.
	159 D	.... Hm hm
	160	.... How much do you drink?

—

161 P .... I don't
162 know.
    [
L8   163 P .. Enough to make me go to sleep at night .... and that's
164 quite a bit.
        [
M9   165 D One or two drinks a day?
166 P O:h no no no humpf it's
167 (more like) ten. ...... at night.
                    [
168 D How many drinks- a night.
169 P At night.
170 D ....
171 Whaddya ta- What type of drinks? .... I (...)-
                                [
172 P Oh vodka. .. yeah
173 vodka and ginger ale.
174 D .... How long
175 have you been drinking that heavily?
                        [
L9   176 P .... Since
177 I've been married.
                [
M10 178 D .... How long is that?
179 P (giggle..) Four
180 years.
            [
L10 181 P (giggle) huh Well I started out with before then I was
182 drinkin beer but u:m I had a job and I was .... ya know ......
183 had more things on my mind and ya know I like- but since I
184 got married I been in and out of jobs and everything so ....
185 I- I have ta have somethin to go to sleep.
186 D ...... Hm:m
187 P ....
188 .... I mean I'm not gonna- ...... It's either gonna be pills
189 or it's gonna be .. alcohol .... and uh alcohol seems
190 to satisfy me moren than pills do .... They don't seem to get
191 strong enough .... pills that I have got I had- I do have
192 Valium .... but they're two milligrams .... and

193   that's supposed to quiet me down during the day but it doesn't.

M11   194   D

195   .... How often do you take them?

(End of excerpt)

CHAPTER 5

Attending to the Voice of the Lifeworld: Alternative Practices and Their Functions

Introduction

There has been a progressive movement in the two preceding chapters through several related, but distinct, modes of analysis and interpretation. The path led from an initial description of the typical structure of unremarkable interviews, through an interpretation of the functional significance of this structure to maintain physicians' control of the discourse, to a critique of the domination of clinical practice by a technological model of medicine. The approach used in the first phase of the study led to a series of findings that emphasized the physicians' control over the organization and content of medical interviews. The basic structure of the interview, reflecting physicians' patterns of questioning with the associated control of the turn-taking system, gave these interviews an appearance of coherence and fluency. The smooth surface of the discourse was occasionally disrupted by patients, usually by introducing content referring to their personal circumstances or the meaning of illness in their lives. Physicians tended to repair these disruptions rapidly to regain control of the interview.

This was the picture that emerged from the first set of analyses. Critical reflection on these preliminary findings and their underlying methodological and theoretical assumptions revealed the dependence of the approach on the biomedical perspective of physicians. This led to a new approach in which the interpretive thrust of earlier analyses was interrupted by making the patient's account the center of inquiry. This shift in focus allowed for the development of an interpretation of clinical discourse that did not depend on the technical perspective of physicians or the assumptions of the biomedical model. A revised description of medical interviews was provided through new transcription rules more consistent with the new approach. Analyses focused on the distinction between the voices of the lifeworld and of medicine as representing different and incompatible ways of organizing and thinking about experience. The struggle between these voices, and the difficulties faced by patients in presenting a coherent account of their problems, emerged as prominent characteristics in medical interviews. Earlier findings on dominance by the voice of medicine and its apparent consequence, the well-structured and orderly surface of discourse, were shown to conceal disruption and disorganization at a deeper level as patients' efforts to provide meaningful and coherent accounts of their problems were disrupted.

The quality of the physician-patient relationship suggested in the earlier analyses and explained at a deeper level in the new approach, is captured well in John Berger's astute and perceptive essay on the development of a country doctor's views of his patients and practice. In the early years, "He had no patience with anything except emergencies or serious illness. ... He dealt only with crises in which he was the central character; or, to put it another way, in which the patient was *simplified* by the degree of his physical dependence on the doctor" (1969, p. 55). Berger portrays a significant change over time in the doctor's view of medicine as primarily focused on life-and-death emergencies with the doctor engaged in heroic action to an "intimation that the patient should be treated as a total personality, that illness is frequently a form of expression rather than a surrender to natural hazards" (p. 62).

The "simplified" construction of patient-physician relationships is easily recognized in the "unremarkable" interviews examined earlier. Its implications are evident in the disruption of patients' contextual accounts of their problems and in the struggle between the voice of the lifeworld and of medicine. Berger's description of one physician's change in orientation carries an important message; that this relationship may take other forms that derive from an "intimation" that patients and their illnesses may be treated in terms of their "total" personalities. In this chapter, I will describe some of the ways in which physicians may move in this direction through increased attentiveness to the voice of the lifeworld.

Preliminary questions for analysis may be posed as follows: What are the features of a medical interview in which both the voices of the lifeworld and of medicine remain active and audible? How is such discourse achieved and maintained? It may be recalled that earlier analyses led to the conclusion that the two voices express distinctly different "provinces of meaning" (Schutz, 1962) or "modes of consciousness" (Habermas, 1970). Further, both Schutz and Habermas imply that translation without distortion between the two voices may be impossible. Nonetheless, we all recognize that medical interviews run their course, pass through certain typical phases, and reach some point of termination. Patients and physicians continue to talk together and, despite their difficulties, often appear to arrive at some measure of agreement and understanding.

Evidence from earlier analyses suggests that the principal mechanism through which these interviews are sustained as continuing discourse is the dominance of the voice of medicine. The voice of the lifeworld is often disregarded and suppressed and finds expression only in occasional and rapidly-repaired interruptions. The surface appearance of "agreement" and organization found in unremarkable interviews reflects the fact that patients are pressed to speak in the one voice that will be heard. In this chapter, I will be looking for an alternative solution, one in which both voices can be heard. I argued earlier that the triumph of the technocratic consciousness, as embodied in the dominant voice of medicine, had as its consequence the dehumanization of clinical practice. The aim of this chapter is to describe the features of an alternative mode of discourse to retrieve the possibilities of a more humane medical interview.

One caveat is in order about the work reported below. As will be seen, the physician is again the center of attention. This is not intended as a reversal of the position developed in the last chapter where the voice of medicine was interrupted by analyses that emphasized patients and the voice of the lifeworld. Rather, restoring the physician to prominence reflects both the limitations of the materials and the aim of demonstrating how physicians, even under current circumstances, may engage in an alternative form of clinical practice. It is difficult to find examples of medical interviews that are not physician-dominated, and other investigators have noted this problem. Byrne and Long (1976), for example, reported that their corpus of more than 1500 interviews did not include one instance that followed a "consultation" model, a type of clinical orientation that to some degree overlaps our notion of responsiveness to patients' lifeworld concerns. Hauser (1981), in his review of studies of patient-physician interaction, concluded that the pattern of physician dominance was a consistent and general finding.

On the whole, the sample of interviews used in this study do not deviate strikingly from those reported in other studies. However, it is important to bear in mind that there are serious limitations in the sources of data. Such studies, my own included, tend to focus almost exclusively on "single-shot interviews," often first meetings between a patient and physician where the primary aim is diagnosis of a current complaint. Excluded from these studies are instances of long-term clinical management of a chronic illness. Also excluded are instances where either the practitioner encourages a more active role or the patient has learned to take a more active role. The women's health movement, for example, has placed considerable emphasis on the importance for women to gain control over their medical care and treatment. Various organizational and educational efforts have been directed to this end (see Ruzek, 1978). Thus, limitations of the health care system, of typical forms of practice, and of the data base in investigations of medical interviews all place constraints on analysis and interpretation. I shall return to these issues in the concluding section of this chapter.

In view of these limitations, the principal example used in the following analyses will not be intended as exemplary. Nonetheless, it will serve to illustrate how clinical practice may have different qualities when physicians are more attentive to and begin to speak in the voice of the lifeworld.

The Functions of Discourse: A Framework for Analysis

In order to develop these analyses in a methodic and systematic way, I will draw upon and adapt the three-part classification of language functions proposed by Halliday (1966, 1967, 1968, 1970, 1973; Kress, 1976). He specifies three essential functions defined as follows: (a) Textual—the construction of situationally relevant connected stretches of discourse; (b) Interpersonal—the expression and regulation of social roles; and (c) Ideational—the development of referential meaning. At the linguistic level of clauses and sentences, these functions are linked to structural components of a specific theory of grammar. Although Halliday was interested primarily in analyzing the linguistic options for constructing clauses, he and Hasan also applied his model to the problem of cohesion in texts, that is, to the ways in which sentences are connected together (Halliday & Hasan, 1976). I shall be extending the model still further in an attempt to analyze the stretches of discourse constructed by two speakers.

Halliday's approach has a number of advantages as a point of departure. First, the model is comprehensive and includes aspects of language that are usually separated and studied in isolation from each other as, for example, in work using the more traditional and well-known classification of semantics, syntax, and pragmatics as different domains of linguistic theory. Distinctions between a theory of grammar and a theory of meaning, between structure and content, and between linguistic competence and linguistic performance are familiar contrasting pairs in the latter approach. Since Halliday's theory of grammar is addressed to the description and analysis of ''language in use,'' his model provides a place for all of these aspects of language and directs our attention to the ways in which they are both differentiated from and related to each other.

Second, Halliday views language as a system of options with expressed language representing choices made by speakers among various sets and networks of available features. Serious attention is given to the significance of the choices made that are represented in the text itself. This is in accord with an interest in the function and significance of systematically different choices by different speakers, such as I have found in analyses of the talk of physicians and patients.

In extending and applying Halliday's model, I will examine separately the ways in which the three functions are expressed and carried by particular features of discourse. Emphasis will be placed on differences between the types of interviews discussed earlier, those dominated by the voice of medicine and those in which the voice of the lifeworld receives more attention and achieves relatively greater prominence. The central question will be: What are the characteristics of such discourse and how do they differ from the "standard" medical interview? I will first analyze the Textual function, that is, the ways in which continuity and cohesion of discourse is maintained in different ways in the two different types of interviews. Second, I will turn to the Interpersonal function and the forms of relationship between physicians and patients as speakers. Finally, I will examine issues of references and meaning, Halliday's Ideational function, and particularly the problem of the transformation of meaning.

Textual Function: Coherence and Continuity of Discourse

For Halliday and Hasan (1976),[1] cohesion refers to ways in which sentences are connected to each other that allow readers (or hearers) to recognize a stretch of language as text rather than nontext. They specify and elaborate subvariants of five types of cohesion. Four are grammatical: reference, substitution, ellipsis, and conjunction; and the fifth is lexical. Each instance of a cohesive connection is referred to as a "tie." For example, the use of a pronoun in a second sentence, standing for a noun or noun phrase in a first sentence, is a tie by substitution; an unexpanded answer to a Yes/No question is a tie by ellipsis in that the subject-predicate clause of the question is presupposed in the answer.

Although the "texts" in this study are transcripts of recorded exchanges between speakers, as compared to the written texts examined by Halliday and Hasan, the various types of cohesive ties are abundantly evident. The use of ellipsis in patient responses is omnipresent, as in the following example:

D Have you ever had rheumatism bone disease or syphilis?
P No.

Ties through reference are also prominent:

P Wel:l when I eat something wrong.
D How- How soon after you eat it.

Halliday and Hasan's framework may be used heuristically to develop an approach to the study of cohesion in discourses con-

---

[1] See also the use of their model of cohesion in a study of the speech of schizophrenic patients by Rochester and Martin (1979).

structed by two speakers. Nonetheless, a significant difference between their work and the problems of cohesion in natural discourse must be recognized. Their data consists of intuitively-understood examples of connected discourse; they either construct hypothetical examples to display a particular type of cohesion or select written passages that they "know" to be cohesive. A core assumption, that they do not reflectively examine or analyze, is that we as readers/hearers can recognize cohesive texts and distinguish them from noncohesive lists of sentences. This is similar to the assumption, in other theories of grammar, that the "grammaticality" of a sentence is intuitively understood by native speakers; Halliday and Hasan have simply extrapolated this assumption to the level of discourse. The central task they pursued is the description and specification of various types of "ties" that are present in texts already known to be cohesive.

We face a different problem; the "cohesiveness" of discourse cannot be assumed but must be discovered. I have already demonstrated a lack of cohesion in medical interviews in the sense that meanings are not shared. The voices of the lifeworld and of medicine represent different provinces of meaning and different structures of logic, cognition, and relevance. Yet, as I have noted before, the interview continues and physicians and patients find ways to speak together despite the gap between them. The specific aim of this chapter is to discover how a discourse is developed and maintained that achieves some degree of "audibility" and understanding between the contending voices, and, therefore, to specify particular mechanisms of cohesion for such a discourse.

Although cohesion was not a central topic in earlier analyses, several features of medical interviews were described that appear to serve the function of constructing a cohesive "text." These provide a preliminary list of discourse-cohesion processes.

First, there is the basic three-part structural unit of the standard medical interview: physician question–patient response–physician question. As was discussed earlier, this unit functions in two ways. Each exchange has a cohesive unity that comes from the demand quality of questions, the adjacency pair structure of questions and answers, and the second physician question that is a specific instance of the questioner's "right to the floor."[2] Second, by linking

---

[2] On a questioner's "reserved right to talk again" and other rules of conversational sequence, see the early observations of Sacks (1972).

one exchange cycle with another, the physician's second question ties the separate exchanges together to form the extended discourse of the full interview.

While the form of these statements as questions and responses provides structural cohesion, the type of question asked and the topics of inquiry produce another type of cohesion, that of reference or meaning. Halliday and Hasan distinguish between cohesion through structure and cohesion through "register," respectively, they are the linguistic and extralinguistic contexts of relevance that ground the meaning of each sentence and relate sentences meaningfully to each other (1976). The particular register of medical interviews is expressed in the overwhelming tendency of physicians to ask response-constraining questions of the Yes/ No or restricted Wh- type and to follow a logic of inquiry based on the biomedical model. As I showed earlier, this emphasizes abstract, objective, and decontextualized features of patients' problems; this emphasis provides the recognizable quality of the standard register of medical interviews.

Finally, there is the cohesion produced by the dominance of the medical voice. Disruptions or breakdowns in the basic structure or deviations from medically appropriate topics are corrected or repaired so that the cohesion of the interview is maintained on the basis of the single register of the voice of medicine. These are particularly interesting devices since they appear on the surface of the discourse as examples of a lack of cohesion, yet cohesion in meaning is maintained at a deeper level. Among the various ways in which this cohesion of dominant register is maintained are the following: (a) lack of explicit acknowledgement of patients' responses, particularly to aspects of the response falling outside the boundaries of the biomedical model; (b) lack of explicit transitional terms or phrases by physicians to introduce their next questions, again particularly evident when patients have introduced non-medically relevant content; and (c) physicians' interruptions of patients' statements, usually with a return to their own line of questioning as a way of indicating the relevance or nonrelevance of certain topics and contents.

Our first task in this analysis is to locate instances that contrast with the ways noted above through which cohesion is maintained in interviews dominated by the voice of medicine. I have suggested that cohesion in both structure and register is provided by physicians, as questioners and topic-initiators, and by the ways in which patients' responses in a register representing the voice of the lifeworld are ignored and discounted. Our questions are: What are the alternative forms of questions that invite and encourage responses in a patient's register? What are the ways in which patients' statements are acknowledged? How are explicit transitions made between topics, and particularly, between two voices?

Examples will be drawn primarily from one interview that seems different in quality from others examined earlier. The physician appears to be more attentive to the voice of the lifeworld. A closer examination may help us to specify some alternative ways in which a cohesive discourse may be developed, ways that do not depend on the dominance of the medical register. This is an initial interview between a male physician and a 76-year-old woman who has come to the clinic because she has been "having weak spells" that are not responding to treatments recommended by her personal physician. The interview opens with the excerpt in Transcript 5.1.

Open-ended Questions. I proposed earlier that through their use of response-constraining questions physicians control both the structure and content of interviews. With reference to the particular discourse function of textual cohesion, I also noted that the pervasiveness of questions of this type maintains cohesion through the dominant register of the voice of medicine. Similar to other physicians, this physician also asks Yes/No and restricted Wh- questions, as in "Where- where- where are you from?" at the end of this excerpt. However, he also asks open-ended questions. In addition, he allows the patient to continue without interruption giving full and elaborate answers to his questions.

Physicians' initial questions in medical interviews tend to be somewhat more open than those asked in the more focused diagnostic phase. For that reason, the opening questions in this excerpt may not stand out as particularly remarkable: "Now what brings you .... to the clinic today?" nor his restatement after her initial response, "What happened that made you come to the screening clinic?" Nonetheless, these questions are relatively more open than those found in more typical interviews. For example, another physician begins with "Could you tell me what the trouble was that made you come in here?" Another opens by asking: "What's the problem?" These latter questions already constrain the appropriateness of the patient's response to those categories of "trouble" or "problem." I would suggest that question stems such as "What brings you" and "What happened"

Transcript 5.1

W:11.110/01

001 D Now what brings you .... to the clinic toda:y?
002   I notice that you haven't been here .... according to
                                    [
003 P   Well I was in last we:ek.
004 D   = your record.
005 D   Oh really.
006 P   I was in here two weeks ago.
007 D   Two weeks
008   ago. Okay. Yeah. This ull-
                [
009 P   (...)
010 D   Right. An:d what-
                                        [
011 P   But I came
012   to screening.
013 D   What happened that made you come to the
014   screening clinic.
            [
015 P   Well uh .... first of all I'd had a lotta trouble
016   with my stomach which I .. thought probably was uh .. from
017   my gall bladder condition and I *know* I was supposed to stay
                                        [
018 D   Hm hm
019 P   on a diet and I wasn't too careful .... in the last few
020   months. .... For about two years I uh lived (laughter) right
021   on it. ...... And then I went . myself back on it ....
022   and uhm that improved some but the veinin in my right legs
023   are beginning to bother me terribly. .... And uhm
024   .... Well I'll- First . of all I had been to a .
025   doctor about a month or so ago .. and he said that my pressure
026   was ...... high .... and I took some pa- pills I brought
027   them in with me because Mr. Holloway asked me what I was
028   takin and I said I didn't know. And (...)-
                                        [
029 D   Oh good I'm glad you
030   brought them in.

```
031 P                    And after .... a we:ek I called the doctor
032      cause I felt wor:se . and he said ta cut down . a half of a
033      pill instead of . the whole one.
034 D                              Hm hm
035 P                                        And then the following
036      week I went back-
                        [
037 D                    How- How did you feel worse. What- What
038      was going on ( ... )?
                [
039 P      Well I was having weak spells. I think that was probably
040      what started me to come in here in the first place (laughter)
041      because I got to the point where I thought I wasn't gettin
042      any help ........ locally .. you know ...... and where you had
043      my records and all my troubles (laughter).
                            [          [
044 D                          Right .. Where- Where- Where are
045      you from?
```

are less constraining as they do not specify particular categories for patient responses.

In typical interviews, we found a pattern in which successive questions on the same topic became increasingly specific and constraining. This physician's use of two successive open-ended questions is in marked contrast to that pattern. His second question is as open as the first in not specifying a response category. However, it is a "redoing" of his first question including explicit acknowledgement of the patient's correction to his comment on when she had last been to the clinic (she reports having been to "screening" "last week" or "two weeks ago"). He does not press her towards accuracy on the time of that visit, which is the direction we would expect to be taken in a typical interview. Rather, he incorporates the content of her response and focuses his rephrased opening question on the event itself. He does not rephrase his question into a form that is more response-constraining. Thus, he sustains the cohesion of this first series of exchanges by tying his second question back to his first question and to the patient's response.

After asking her "What happened," he listens. He allows the

patient to tell her story at some length without interruption. There is only one "Hm hm" attention signal and no comment during several pauses, even though it is evident from the text that the patient rambles and introduces a number of apparently different topics such as her gall bladder infection, her diet and compliance with it, "veinin" in her legs, a previous visit to a doctor, high blood pressure, and her prescribed medication. At the end of her relatively long account, he does not press her to be more specific nor select one of the topics for further questioning but makes a positive assessment to her report of bringing in her pills for identification: "Oh good I'm glad you brought them in."

After a further statement by the patient about her condition, the physician asks another open-ended question using her words as the object clause: "How did- How did you feel worse?" There is a brief pause, indicating that the patient does not respond immediately, and he follows up with another open-ended question, "What- what was going on." Again, although the shift within his utterance from an open-ended, but focused, question to an even more open-ended question may appear to be a rather insignificant feature of complex discourse, it must be placed in the context of earlier analyses which pointed to a pattern of increasing specificity of questions as physicians proceeded through each subtopic in the interview. I shall return to the functional significance of the physician's use of his patients' words in a later section on reference and the ideational function of language.

In terms of frequency, open-ended questions do not constitute a high proportion of this physician's utterances. However, they appear at various points throughout the interview, and their occurrence is striking since such questions rarely appear in the typical interviews analyzed earlier. For example, after the initial exchange recorded in Transcript 5.1, the patient continues with her account of why she has come to the clinic; she refers at several points to "having weak spells." After her repetition of this problem, the physician asks, "Hm hm How would you describe this spell?" This question, using the patient's own terms, requests further elaboration; this dual quality characterizes this physician's mode of discourse. He maintains this openness for further elaboration to the end of the interview. As he moves towards the close of the interview, and after the usual complement of a medical history, physical examination, and recommendations for further tests, he asks, "Is there anything that .... we haven't talked about that's bothering you at all? Or anything like that?"

It is important to look more closely at how a particular type of discourse cohesion is developed through the way in which this physician asks open-ended questions, a cohesion that ties together utterances of both speakers. Figure 5.1 abstracts some of the central components of this stretch of the interview to highlight both the features and location of this series of open-ended questions.

I have already noted that his second question restates his opening question, but it acknowledges the patient's correction of his information which is a significant difference. The patient has qualified her correction, "But," thus marking her awareness that where she had gone, "to screenin," is different from where she is now.

In response to the physician's "What happened" question, she reports on her symptoms, previous medical visits, and continued difficulties. Her account, presented in Transcript 5.1, although diffuse and scattered in the topics to which she refers, is rather tightly tied together by temporal and causal conjunctions and connecting phrases. Earlier, by abstracting the flow of topics from her talk and listing them independently—gall bladder, veinin, and

Figure 5.1 Open-Ended Questions: Schematic Summary

D: What brings you to the clinic today?

       D: I notice you haven't been here.

       P: I was in last week/two weeks ago.

          D: Two weeks ago/Right.

       P: But I came to screenin.

D: What happened that made you come to the screening clinic.

       P: Lotta trouble

        been to a doctor month or so ago

        took some pills

        brought them in with me

          D: Good glad you brought them

       P: After a week I felt worse

D: How did you feel worse. What was going on?

---

so forth—I concluded that she "rambles." However, she connects them together by introducing the topics in her main clauses by phrases such as "first of all," "and he said," "and after a week," "cause," "and he said," "I think that was probably what started me," "because I got to the point," and "where you had my records." The structure of meanings provided by these ways of tying the elements of her story together is the same as we found earlier when analyzing the logical and cognitive structuring of experiences expressed in the voice of the lifeworld. It is organized in terms of temporal and causal contingencies with the patient herself as the center and focus of events.

The physician has allowed the story to unfold in the patient's own words. Its coherence as a structure of lifeworld meanings has not been disrupted. It is in this context that his open-ended questions, at the end of her account, take on their particular significance for the cohesiveness of the discourse as a conversation between speakers. In asking, "How- How did you feel worse," he ties his question lexically to that part of her story that appears to be its climactic point and, at the same time, is the answer to his earlier question, "What happened that made you come to the screening clinic." Thus, his two questions are tied together through explicit reference to the patient's answer. Of equal importance is the fact that since the patient's statement, "And after .... a *we:ek* I called the doctor cause I felt worse" is integral to her story, connected meaningfully to the other elements, the physician's question both confirms and enters into the cohesiveness of her account. In other words, because the patient has come to the point in her narrative where she "felt worse," and has imparted related events leading to that point the physician's focusing his attention on this element does not abstract and isolate it from its context. Rather the full context is absorbed into his question and retains its relevance.

His succeeding specification question, "What- What was going on (...)?" serves an additional function. By ties of substitution, in Halliday and Hasan's terms, "going on" represents both the patient's "felt worse" and the "What happened" in his earlier question. Thus, his questions complete a circle of meaning.

The significance of the cohesion-producing function of this physician's use of open-ended questions, often with the patient's own words as their object clauses, may be more fully appreciated by contrasting it with typical sequences found in our earlier analyses of unremarkable and interrupted interviews. For example, in an interview reported in Chapter 3, we found the following exchange pairs:

W:02.014

> P ... And a cough. And a cough .. which is the most irritating aspect.
>
> [
>
> D Okay (hh) us any fever?
>
> P ... Now (there's) mostly cough
>
>   [
>
> D   What about the nasal dis-charge? Any
>
> P There's been nothing on the hankerchief.
>
>   [
>
> D   hm hm   Okay. ... (hh) Do you have any pressure around your eyes?

I described these interviews as organized through the dual function of physician's questions that terminated prior units, often with an explicit assessment, "Okay" or "hm hm," and initiated next units. I also noted that in addition to the control of the turn-taking structure through the act of questioning, the physician's control of content was ensured through closed-ended Yes/No types of questions that did not refer back explicitly to prior responses but introduced new content to which the patient was expected to reply. These examples, with content coming solely from the physician—"fever," "nasal discharge," "pressure around your eyes"—were clearly different in function from the open-ended "How did you feel worse," in the text just reviewed. In the earlier interview, cohesiveness in structure derived from the physician's control of turn-taking, and in content from the register of the voice of medicine.

In the second stage of analysis, in which I focused on ways that the voice of medicine interrupted the voice of the lifeworld, I pointed to the fragmented and disjointed nature of the interviews. It was difficult to extract a patient's story as a coherent account since physicians followed a different logic and used their position as questioners to control the organization and content of the interview. Cohesion of meaning in terms of patient's lifeworlds, when it appeared, was primarily a function of their efforts to connect parts of their accounts while simultaneously attempting to provide adequate answers to physicians' questions. For example, in the following excerpt, from an interview presented in Chapter 4, the patient responds to the question about whether she had blood clots with each of her childhood ulcers but then connects that with her current symptoms and offers that connection as the reason for her coming to the clinic. The physician does not refer directly to the content of her statement, beyond a minimal assessment, and introduces a new topic with a closed-ended Yes/No question.

W:13.121/0

    P Yes. There were blood clots.
    D   .... With the first one or
       the second one?
    P   Both. .... In fact this is last
                                     [
    D   Hm hm
    P I- that's what ya know, that's- my other one started that
       way.
    D   Hm hm. Did you have an X-ray at that time?

Further analyses of how the physician interrupted the patient's account in this interview showed how the meaning of her statements, in terms of her lifeworld situation, was consistently ignored by the physician as he transformed her response into objective, biomedically-relevant terms. For example, after she mentions that her "sour stomach" symptom comes after she eats something wrong, the physician asks:

W:13.121/0

    D How- How soon after you eat it?
    P We:ll ...... probably an hour .... maybe less.
                                     [
    D   About an hour?
    P Maybe less. .... I've cheated and I've been drinking
       which I shouldn't have done.
    D   .... Does drinking make it
       worse?

And later in the interview:

D .... How much do you drink?

P   .... I don't
know. ... Enough to make me go to sleep at night ....
and that's quite a bit.

D   One or two drinks a day?

In neither instance does the physician tie his question to the central content of the patient's statement, her "cheating" or her drinking "enough" to go to sleep. I argued that in this precise sense, her account is interrupted by the voice of medicine. For that reason, the discourse lacks the cohesiveness found in the interview excerpt presented above in which the physician's questions help to sustain and develop the coherent meaning of the patient's account.

These analyses of the cohesiveness function of open-ended questions, and analyses of other functions to be described in the following sections, have a different direction of movement than those reported in earlier chapters. In the latter, I began with features of talk and then built an interpretation on the basis of findings. For example, I developed the concept of the voices of the lifeworld and of medicine on the basis of specific differences between the utterances of physicians and patients, of disjunctions between them, and of disruptions in the discourse. In the present analysis, I began from the other end, starting with an overall impression that this interview was different in quality from typical and "unremarkable" interviews. I then examined certain details of the talk in order to document and test the initial impression.

In a sense, the methodological strategy is similar to that used before; I have interrupted my previous mode of analysis. At the same time, I have relied on earlier findings and interpretations of the different voices. That is, the initial impression of this interview as different in quality reflected an unspecified and preliminary understanding of this discourse as representing a different relationship between the two voices than had been found before. This approach is consistent with the aim of the present analyses: to locate alternative types of clinical discourse in which the physician is more attentive to the voice of the lifeworld and, further, to specify the ways in which this difference in attentiveness is realized in speech. Thus, the analyses have progressed in a dialectical, rather than in a linear, course with each new analysis interrupting, or negating, the previous one to further enlarge our understanding of clinical work.

A second point that requires explicit comment has to do with my interpretation of the function of open-ended questions. This particular form of speech was selected for close examination for two closely-related reasons. First, it was clear that in typical interviews physicians' use of closed-end response-constraining types of questions was pervasive; second, the physician in this interview appeared to use open-ended questions relatively more frequently. I believe that a comparison of typical interviews with this interview, and others like it, would be likely to show that a relatively higher ratio of open- to closed-end questions exist in the latter. However, such a comparison is not the primary intent of these analyses nor does it constitute a recommendation for future studies.

In interpreting how this physician's use of open-ended questions produced a certain type of cohesiveness of discourse, I have already suggested, though not elaborated the view, that the use of this form of question is not in itself sufficient for understanding the difference in quality between interviews. A research strategy that coded open- and closed-end questions, and then counted and compared their relative frequencies, would not lead to the interpretation developed here. Rather, it has been necessary to locate each use of an open-ended question in the context of the patient-physician discourse to (a) examine connections between his questions and the content and internal cohesiveness of patients' accounts, and (b) to explore how the form of question combines with attentiveness to the voice of the lifeworld to produce a type of cohesiveness based on a different register than the voice of medicine. In this approach, instead of counting occurrences, the aim is to determine the ways that open-ended questions function contextually, within the flow of meaning as it is constructed through the discourse.

Transitions Between Speakers and Voices.   In their work on cohesion, Halliday and Hasan focus primarily on connections between clauses through certain types of ties such as substitution and reference. Ties between utterances of different speakers, as was shown in the previous section, can also describe the cohesiveness of discourse between speakers. This approach, however, is not particularly useful for analysis of the problem of transition between voices and the ways in which this is accomplished.

In earlier analyses of the basic structure of interviews dominated by the voice of medicine, and in further analyses of interruptions of each voice by the other, I stressed the disjunction between the voices and the consequent fragmentation of meaning. This was evident in many ways—in the frequency with which physicians interrupted patients' accounts, in the lack of explicit acknowledgement of patients' responses, in shifts to new topics without explicit transitional comments, and in disruptions of fluent speech for both patient and physicians when new topics were introduced or a new voice entered the discourse.

I also pointed out that efforts to produce a smoother transition between turns, or to maintain cohesiveness of an account, were almost entirely initiated by patients. Thus, in the example used above from W:13.121/01, in which the patient responds to the physician's question about whether she had blood clots with her first or second ulcer, she attempts by her response to tie her previous medical history to her present symptoms and to her reason for coming to the clinic: "Both .... In fact this is last time too .... That's why I came here because I- I- that's what ya know that's- my other one started that way." In the course of her statement she is interrupted by the physician's "Hm hm" and at the end of her statement, after a similar minimal acknowledgement, he goes on to another topic: "Did you have an X-ray at that time?"

The omission by physicians of explicit transitional terms and phrases in typical interviews and the resulting fragmentation of discourse alert us to search for types of transition comments that might function to maintain continuity and cohesion across different speakers and voices. For example, are there more adequate ways through which physicians acknowledge patients' responses and effect smoother transitions between the voices of the lifeworld and of medicine? In examining the function of open-ended questions, I have already described one way in which a physician may maintain coherence of meaning across turns, by using the patient's own words in his question. I will now describe other devices serving the same function.

Whereas omission of explicit acknowledgement of patients' statements is a prominent feature of earlier interviews, the physician in the case under review often directly acknowledges the patient's response and sometimes adds a positive assessment of her reported action. Thus, as seen in Transcript 5.1, the patient ends her long response to his first question with a reference to pills she has been taking: "... and I took some pa- pills I brought them in with me because Mr. Holloway asked me what I was taking and I said I didn't know. And ..." The physician responds: "Oh good I'm glad you brought them in." Later, at the end of the excerpt, he asks where she is from; this is a relevant question as the patient has just made a distinction between not getting help "locally" and deciding to "come in here." The exchange continues as follows:

W:11.110/01

```
         [          [
D  Ri:ght .. Where- Where- Where are you from?
P                                    Revere. (laughter)
D                                                From
   Rever:e?
P          Yea:h.
D                 It's kinda hard for you to get in? It's-
                                                [
P                                    No not
   too bad no ... and so I thought ya know well this was the
   thing to do because you um had my records in here
                                    [
D                                    Hm hm
```

In both instances, the physician responds directly and explicitly to the meaning in the patient's responses. His direct acknowledgement contrasts sharply with the strings of "Hm hms" and "Okays" found in other interviews. Those utterances appeared to serve the primary purpose of holding the turn so that the physician could proceed with the next question. In the second exchange above, the physician goes beyond acknowledgement and responds in the voice of the lifeworld. He takes into account the patient's circumstances: "It's kinda hard for you to get in?"

Later, after the initial review of her symptoms, he offers a preliminary diagnosis of anemia and states the reason for and the aim of what he plans to do. The exchange, reported in Transcript 5.2, continues with comments by both about her age.

Again, the physician responds directly to her concerns about

Transcript 5.2

W:11.110/01

001 D And uh your urine is fine. So you don't have any problems
                                                        [
002 P   Hm hm
003 D there. .. Let me ask you a few more questions though-
                                                        [
004 P   Hm hm
005 D I- I think .... the reason for your weakness and dizziness
006   most likely is gonna turn out that- .. that your . anemia
007   can account for this and what .... I think we should do ..
008   is to find out now why you're anemic and what's .... happening
                                                  [
009 P   Hm hm
010 D to make you have low blood all of a sudden.
011 P   Hm hm
012 D   So that uh ..
013   we can fix ya up ..
                         [
014 P   Hm hm
015 D   cause I think ya still- you look pretty
016   healthy.
017 P   Cause my- .. yeah (laughing) cause my age is (...)-
                                        [
018 D   and uh
019 P going against me a little bit.
                         [
020 D   O:h you don't- . you don't look seventy six.
021 P But I'm never- really haven't felt-
                    [
022 D   You don't look seventy six at all. You're
023   still pretty.
024 P   Yeah I've been very active and-
                                     [[
025 D   Uhm uhm Huh huh Good.
026   Have you . had any *nau*sea or vomiting at all?

---

an important aspect of her life circumstances, her age, and re-
assures her with a comment that is unusual in its personal quality
in medical interviews, "You're still pretty." I will return in a later
section to the personal tone of this physician's comments and
their function in establishing a relationship that is less hierarchical,
impersonal, and objective than is found in more typical interviews.
Here, I am focusing on ways in which his direct acknowledgement
of the patient's concerns, often with reassurance and in the voice
of the lifeworld, serves to maintain both structural continuity and
referential coherence in the discourse.

The contrast with unremarkable and physician-dominated interviews must be kept in mind. This physician does not respond
to her remark about her age by ignoring it as nonmedically relevant, or by a minimum assessment such as "Hm hm," or by an
immediate repair of her interruption of the voice of medicine by
a next question on her symptoms. Rather, he responds in the voice
of the lifeworld and the exchange has an expressive and slightly
teasing quality.

Another feature of more typical interviews that made them appear fragmented and disjointed was the absence of transitional
phrases. Physicians did not introduce their next questions even
when they appeared to be on unrelated topics, they did not explicitly connect them to patients' prior responses, nor did they
explain what they were going to do next. This physician's first
utterance, in the above excerpt, is an example of a more adequate
transition; after summarizing his impressions, he goes on by using
the polite form of a request for permission: "Let me ask you a
few more questions though-." Such utterances have a dual function: they summarize what has gone before and anticipate what
is to come at the next point in the interview. Thus, he ties together
different parts of the interview, but in ways that are not captured
by Halliday and Hasan's list of cohesive ties.

At other points he connects his comments and questions to
information already elicited from the patient: "Okay. . Fine.
.... problems that I went through going through your-
through your chart here." He refers back explicitly to information
the patient provided at earlier points in the interview. For example:
"Right. .... Now what you mentioned to me now something about
your leg .. phlebitis that you had . do you have something now
that's causing you some problems or-."

At one point he asks whether physicians she had seen earlier
took blood tests:

"D: He didn't take any blood from you or do any tests or anything like that. P: He did nothing. D: Okay. P: Now a long while ago about a year ago I think .... he said I was a little bit anemic."

She continues after another exchange and question:

"P: He- Yes I said it to him and he took blood from my finger but this was quite a long long ago .... and he said everything was fine .... was .. ya know .... I don't know."

Later the physician reports on what was done more recently with a clear though implicit reference to the earlier discussion:

"D: Let me tell you one *thing* that they did draw some blood here [P: Yes.] and I notice that you are anemic and your chromatica is thirty-one .. which is .... about nine or ten points lower than it should be and-".

He goes on to indicate that the results of these tests suggest a preliminary diagnosis of anemia.

The switch within an interview from history taking to a physical examination is often done abruptly, as we have seen, with little preparation or explanation. In contrast, note the following exchange:

W:11.110/01

D Hm hm .... Okay. Good. Why don't you .... get into a johnny if you could.

P   Hm Hm

D   And uh .. we'll examine you. I'm gonna want to do a rectal exam.

P   Hm hm

D   Check your s- stool to see if you have any blood there.

After this exchange, he continues to talk with her about anemia and her other symptoms, the possibility that there might be some internal bleeding, and the problem of her not knowing the names of pills she has been taking. He then repeats his request for her to change for the physical examination: "So why don't you get into a little johnny and I'm gonna run and find out what the name of this pill is." However, they continue to talk about the problem of the unknown pills; she relates at some length an incident where her ignorance about the pills created a problem. He again repeats his earlier request, explaining that he will leave while she is changing.

W:11.110/1

D Okay. Uh .... Okay. Let- Why don't you get
    the johnny on and I'll go out.
                          [
P   Okay
D   And we'll come back in
    and I'll
      [
P   Whadya do . tie it in the back or-
D   Yeah . in the back.

When he returns, he reports: "Yeah I checked these pills," and tells her what they are called and their purpose.

He then reports the results of his physical examination and explains why he will be starting a new line of questioning: "Your stool that I sampled was negative . so there's no blood in it . uh but you are . anemic ... So let me just talk with you ask you a few questions to begin with about that .. You- You cook for yourself?" He also explains an interruption extraneous to the interview: "Okay why don't you get dressed while I answer my page. My little beeper just went off, that means someone wants me on the phone."

At the end of the interview the physician summarizes his impressions and preliminary diagnosis, describes the approach he is going to take, and explains the reasons for tests he has ordered. He then moves into the termination of the interview with a question that is as open-ended as the one with which he began the interview, but which reflects back on what they have talked about. Finally, he ends with a personal comment and a reassuring statement that are consistent with the clinical "line" he has developed over the course of the interview. (See Transcript 5.3.)

Discussion. The Textual function, in Halliday's model of language, refers to the achievement of cohesiveness in a text or discourse. The general aim of this type of functional analysis is to

Transcript 5.3

W:11.110/01

```
001   D   Is there anything that ................... we haven't talked
002       about that's bothering you at all? Or anything like that?
003   P   ............ No (...)
                      [
004   D                    Okay. Fine. Good. So we haven't left too
005       much of anything out . not a lotta headaches or sore throats
                  [
006·  P         Hm hm
007   D   or colds or-
          [
008   P   No.        I used to have terrible headaches (but) haven't
009       had them for years.
010   D                       Haven't had them for years.
011   P                                       Yeah. .. I
012       guess it was tryin to raise a family caused them. (laughter)
013   D   Well I guess seven kids are enough (laughter) to give me a
014       headache anyway I don't know. ................... Okay. Well
015       fine I'll .. get some of this written up and we'll .. get some
016       of your lab tests on underway and .. get you on the road to
017       gettin better.
```

---

describe various ways in which a cohesive text may be constructed. I adopted this approach in order to make a precise and detailed comparison between different types of medical interviews; those dominated by the voice of medicine and those in which the voice of the lifeworld appears to hold a·more central place in the discourse. This work has extended the model by leading to the discovery of different types of cohesiveness and to our finding that ways of developing cohesiveness in discourse between speakers are not limited to syntactic and lexical ties between clauses.

The interview used here as the principal example for comparison with previously-analyzed interviews was not intended, as I noted earlier, to serve as an exemplar of humane interviews nor as an exhibit of best or only ways for producing a different type of cohesiveness. Nonetheless, it was selected on the basis of an initial impression that it had a different quality than those examined earlier. In particular, it appeared that the physician was more attentive to the voice of the lifeworld. Detailed analyses of the Textual function tend to confirm first impressions and suggest how clinical work may be done without exclusive and overwhelming reliance on the voice of medicine.

In earlier interviews, the voice of medicine served as the principal and almost sole basis for the organization of the interview as cohesive discourse. Physicians controlled and directed the conversation through their use of closed-ended questions, abrupt transitions between topics, interruptions of patients' accounts of their problems, and rapid repairs of patient "disruptions" to bring the interview back within the narrow and constrained channel of the voice of medicine. I have shown a variety of ways in which this interview contrasts with earlier ones. This physician explicitly acknowledges the patient's lifeworld concerns and her real-life circumstances, listens with minimum interruption to her account, asks open-ended questions that tie the course of his inquiry to her narrative, provides explanations of what he is going to do and ask next, and uses the patient's own words both to inquire further about her symptoms and to develop their medical implications. The result is a more complex form of cohesiveness that depends on the interchange between voices rather than solely on the voice of medicine. This type of cohesiveness is a joint product of patient and physician. Instead of the interview structure found in our earlier analyses based on the formal features of utterances as questions and responses, the structure of this interview is based on the development of coherent and shared meanings.

The Textual function is one of three functions in Halliday's model. Analyses of the Interpersonal and Ideational functions will be presented in the next two sections; they refer, respectively, to relationships between speakers and to referential meaning.

Interpersonal Function: Communication Roles and Relationships

In Halliday's triad, the Interpersonal function refers to relationships between speakers. He emphasizes the speakers' respective roles in discourse, for example, as questioners and responders. Here, emphasis will instead be placed on the speakers' more general roles vis-a-vis each other, as patients and physicians, and on the particular qualities of this relationship as they are expressed in speech. In functional terms, I will be describing how social and interpersonal relationships are regulated through talk.

A critical postulate of Halliday's model of language is that all functions are accomplished simultaneously, and at every point in the discourse. More sharply put, discourse cannot exist unless it is cohesive, defines speaker relationships, and has a topic or content. It follows that each linguistic feature has multiple functions. Thus, each lexical term, phrase, clause, and utterance "acts" in three different ways in the separate subsystems representing the different organizations of Textual, Interpersonal, and Ideational functions. For that reason, some of the features identified earlier as producing a particular type of cohesiveness in the text may reappear in analysis of other functions and the same stretches of discourse will sometimes be used.

The choice of dimensions for analysis of particular interpersonal subfunctions depends on a general theory of social relationships as well as on an a priori understanding of patient-physician relationships. Many studies of medical care, particularly of role relationships between patients and physicians, rely on Parsons' (1951, Chapter 10) characterization of the basic norms in this relationship as universalistic, affectively neutral, and functionally specific. Although the dimension of authority and issues of power and control are notably absent from Parsons' scheme, these norms seem, at first glance, to be expressed in the behavior of physicians found in earlier analyses of "unremarkable" interviews.

I have already reviewed the results of those analyses, from initial findings of physicians' methods for controlling the organization and content of interviews, to an interpretation of the dominance of the voice of medicine as one expression of the triumph of technocratic consciousness. That summary gives direction and shape to our present task. I will be looking for alternative ways of speaking that yield different relationships between patients and physicians; different from those governed by presumably normative standards that, when analyzed, turn out to reflect ideological assumptions about the legitimacy and appropriateness of dominance by the voice of medicine.

I will again follow the strategy used throughout this work and begin by interrupting Parson's analysis to question its assumptions. This may be done by reconsidering the sense in which physicians' ways of talking can be viewed as expressing ideal norms. Affective neutrality, for example, appears to be present in their mode of impersonal speech and in their general lack of responsiveness to patients' feelings. Evidence of functional specificity in their orientation may be found in their focus on signs and symptoms, in their specific "objective" parameters, and in the isolation of symptoms from patients' more general problems and lifeworld experiences. The context-stripping approach[3] also reflects the application of universalistic standards in that the underlying abstract biomedical model of disease both orients the direction of physicians' questions and provides the basis for their interpretation of the significance of reported problems.

In Parsons' model, these ways of talking are assumed to be normatively-governed and to serve a positive function. He argues that these norms reduce the inherent strains of medical work arising from uncertainties of diagnosis and treatment in situations that are highly charged emotionally. The norms function to protect physicians, on the one hand, from pressures that would undermine their professional stance as objective and neutral and, on the other hand, protect patients from exploitation at a time of heightened vulnerability. In this way, the norms permit physicians to carry out professional tasks that require a high degree of technical competence.

In my view, the norms and functions specified in this model are grounded in a particular ideology about medical work that reinforces relationships expressing the technocratic consciousness. The alternative formulation proposed here is that more responsiveness to patients' experience and feelings, combined with a recognition of the lifeworld contexts of their problems, does not constitute a deviation from "ideal" norms nor does it undermine the possibilities of effective performance of the physician's complex task. Rather, it is a more humane way of practicing medicine.

The transcripts presented earlier are pervaded with instances of affectively neutral, functionally specific, context-stripping questions and responses by physicians. A major point made in the analyses of these interviews was that they consisted almost entirely of such types of utterances. The following, from an earlier interview reported in Chapter 4, shows this general pattern clearly.

---

[3] For a general discussion of context-stripping, with particular reference to the experimental approach to research in the human sciences, see Mishler (1979a).

W:13.121.01

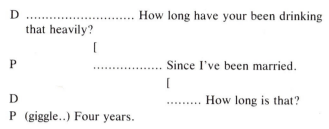

D .... How long have your been drinking
that heavily?

               [

P   .... Since I've been married.

                        [

D   .... How long is that?

P (giggle..) Four years.

It may be recalled that shortly before this exchange, the patient introduces a new topic into the discourse, the problem of her drinking. The physician has asked her what she's been drinking and how much and now asks how long she's been drinking "heavily." The patient's lifeworld response, "Since I've been married," is treated as inadequate, and perhaps, irrelevant. The physician decontextualizes and objectifies the problem by repeating his question "How long," indicating that her response is not an "answer" to his question.

In the present context, I am suggesting that the physician's repetition and rephrasing of his question on the period of time that she has been drinking heavily, "How long is that?" is a realization in speech of the norms specified in Parsons' model of physician-patient role relationships. It is affectively neutral in tone and content as well as in its nonresponsiveness to the affect in the patient's statement. It is functionally specific in its focus on the discrete objective parameter of amount of time rather than on the patient's experience of biographically-relevant time. By rejecting the patient's first response, "Since I've been married," and restating the phrase "How long," the physician asserts universalistic criteria for the adequacy of a response.

A different type of response is illustrated in the following excerpt from the interview used in analyses of cohesiveness. It directly follows the initial exchanges in Transcript 5.1. The patient has recounted her efforts to get effective medical treatment "locally." Her failure has led her to come to the clinic "where you had my records and all my troubles." The physician acknowledges her account and goes on to express concern about the difficulties that this change may present.

W:11.110/01

    [[

D Right. Where- Where are you from?

P   Revere. (laughter)

D   From Rever:e?

P   Yea:h

D   It's

kinda hard for you to get in? It's-

                       [

P   No not too bad no. .... And so I
thought ya know well this was the thing to do because you um
had my records in here. But I had been

             [

D   Hm hm

P having weak spells ...... not- I didn't faint and I wasn't
dizzy.

D   Sure.

In contrast to the other physician's "How long is that?" this physician's comment, "It's kinda hard for you to get in" does not express norms of affective neutrality, functional specificity, and universalism. Moreover, it does not appear that the patient is trying to draw the physician into a nonprofessional relationship, a tendency Parsons suggests is both a principal source of strain in physician-patient relationships and evidence of patients' resistance to the normative requirements of patient and physician roles. Although this physician is expressing concern in what appears to be a non-normative way, his response is nonetheless clinically appropriate and relevant to the work that he and the patient have to do together. Specifically, he is inquiring about difficulties the patient might have as a result of her decision to seek treatment in the clinic. His concern is medically relevant since such difficulties might interfere with the effectiveness of her treatment program.

The following excerpt (Transcript 5.4) is another example of how this physician places a medically-relevant issue in the context of the patient's circumstances thereby establishing a different type of relationship than would exist if he were guided by the norms in Parsons' model. Earlier in the interview, the physician learned that the patient did not know the names of some medications pre-

Transcript 5.4

W:11.110/01

```
001   D   So .. why don't you get into a little johnny and I'm gonna
002       run out and find out what the name of this pill is.
003   P                                         Hm hm
004   D   And I'll tell you. .. What- What you should do .. and uh
005       it's a shame the pharmacist doesn't do it is .... make sure
006       that you know the names of all the pills that you're taking.
                                                [
007   P                                         Yeah.
008   D   It's just a good practical thing cause if something happens
009       .. and you're not in a place where they know you if you can
010       tell them ya know I'm taking .. such and such medicine
011   P                                                      Hm:m
012   D   it's- it's gonna help you to get fixed up quicker so it's
                               [                    [
013   P                        That's true.        Yeah. Hm hm
014   D   just- just a point that I think-
                               [
015   P                        Yeah.
016   D                                      Ya know. It's certainly
017       not crucial now but something for you to know about to be
018       aware of the names of the medicines you take.
```

viously prescribed for her. He has just requested that she get prepared for a physical examination.

It might be supposed that the recommendation to patients that it is important to know the names of their medications would be well within the normative structure of standard medical practice. Nonetheless, physicians are not particularly attentive to this problem. They tend to use technical names of the drugs they prescribe and, in other interviews in this series, they do not make a point of suggesting to patients that they learn and remember the names of drugs. This physician gives a concrete and readily understandable reason why it is important to know "cause if something happens .. and you're not in a place where they know you if you can tell them ya know I'm taking .. such and such medicine (P: Hm:m) it's- it's gonna help you to get fixed up quicker." Shortly after this exchange, the patient confirms her understanding of his cautionary remarks by relating an incident that matches his hypothetical example. She reports that she ran out of pills while visiting her daughter in another state, did not know their names, and indeed ran into difficulty.

At another point, he also takes into account an important aspect of this patient's particular circumstances, that is, her ability to afford the cost of drugs. She reports having been advised by a second physician to stop taking drugs that had been prescribed: "And it costs a fortune to buy pills like that and not use them you know." To which he replies, "Well we'll try ta .. give you cheap pills."

Another more striking departure from the normative stance of affective neutrality and universalism may be found in Transcript 5.2, presented, earlier. The physician has concluded a review of the patient's present symptoms and previous medical care, and offers his preliminary diagnosis of anemia, stating the aims of both the diagnosis and treatment. She calls attention to her age as a critical variable that might qualify the optimism of his remarks that "we can fix ya up" and "you look pretty healthy." She points out, "cause my age is (...)- going against me a little bit." His response to her expressed concern about the effects of her age, "You don't look seventy-six at all. You're still pretty," certainly falls outside the presumably normative boundaries of the proper medical role. However, in terms of the analytic categories used here, he has dropped the voice of medicine and is talking with the patient in the voice of the lifeworld.

Another way this physician occasionally deviates from normative prescriptions is by statements in which he indicates that if he were in the patient's situation he might have the same problems. For example, in the following excerpt, he notes that he would have her symptom if his "chromatica" level was as low as hers: "and I dare say that alone would make me feel a little dizzy" (the term "chromatica" represents my hearing, but it presumably is intended as "hematocrit"). In this way, he affirms their common humanity rather than stressing differences between them due to their special roles in this situation. Through such affirmations, he reduces the social distance between them instead of emphasizing the separation, a separation that is often viewed as an essential feature of physician-patient and other professional expert-client relationships.

W:11.110/01

    D Let me tell you one thing that they did draw some blood
       here
    P   Ye:s
    D   And I notice that you are anemic. Your chro-
       matica is thirty-one .. which is:s about . nine or ten points
       lower than it should be and
                               [
    P   Hm hm Would that cause (...)
                                                  [
    D   and I
       dare say that alone would make me feel a little dizzy.
    P   Yeah.

In Transcript 5.3 presented earlier, the physician terminates the interview by referring back to information the patient gave him about her family and life situation. In addition, he again affirms their similarity as persons rather than their differences as patient and physician. As in the last excerpt above, he frames his comments in personal terms: "Well I guess seven kids are enough (laughter) to give me a headache anyway I don't know."

Discussion.   In examining the particular forms through which the Interpersonal function is realized in the speech of physicians and patients, I have been extending earlier analyses of the Textual function. In the latter, focusing on how cohesiveness of discourse was produced, I showed an interview that had different qualities than were found earlier in typical interviews dominated by the voice of medicine. Here, in contrast, coherence and continuity of discourse are based on the greater reciprocity of voices in the interchange. This different type of cohesiveness is produced primarily through greater attentiveness on the part of the physician to the patient's account of her problem. We found, for example, that he allows her to present an extended account of symptoms and past medical care with minimum interruption, explicitly acknowledges her statements, provides transitions to new topics he initiates, and asks open-ended questions.

The Interpersonal function refers to a second important aspect of language, the type of relationship established between speakers through their forms of speech. I used Parsons' model of normative features of physician and patient roles as a point of reference and contrast to show how a different type of relationship could develop. In the interview examined here, there is evidence of deviation from hypothesized norms of affective neutrality, functional specificity, and universalism. This physician acknowledges the patient's particular circumstances, minimizes the role distance between them, responds to the patient's feelings, and expresses his own feelings.

Despite these deviations from "normative" practice, this discourse very clearly remains an instance of a medical interview. I would argue, therefore, that the qualities of standard and "unremarkable" medical interview are not normative in the sense of a set of universal functional requisites. Rather, they represent the expression of a particular ideology about medical care expressed in the context of medical interviews through the dominance of the voice of medicine. The result is a professional-client relationship that is neutral, distant, abstract. This relationship, realized in the controlling register of the voice of medicine, strips away the life contexts of patients and their problem, treats them as objects, and de-personalizes them. It is clear, from the interview examined here, that appropriate and normative clinical work can proceed with greater reciprocity between the voices of the lifeworld and of medicine.

Beyond that, and of greater significance, attentiveness to the voice of the lifeworld may make it possible both for patients to retain their integrity and humanity and for physicians to achieve satisfactions from their work that do not depend on the "simplification" of patients. These other satisfactions may come, as Berger (1969) poetically states it, when the physician "faces forces which no previous explanation will exactly fit, because they depend upon the history of a patient's particular personality. He tries to keep that personality company in its loneliness" (p. 62).

Ideational Function: Meanings and Their Transformations

Issues of meaning are central to functional analyses of language. Halliday's model directs attention to three types of meaning, that is, to the multiple functions of linguistic features and structures.

Thus, the Textual function refers to the presence and form of cohesiveness in a stretch of text or talk as one type of meaning; qualities and forms of social relationship realized in speech, the Interpersonal function, are a second type of meaning. The Ideational function is not the exclusive domain of meaning but refers to a third type, reference and content. The focus of Ideational analysis is on the topics of discourse, on "What" is being talked about.

Hauser, in his review of studies and observations of interaction between patients and physicians (1981), concludes that there are repeated findings of faulty and inadequate communication. Investigators refer to "gaps," "distortions," and "misunderstandings." This is not surprising in view of the problems we found in analyses of standard and unremarkable medical interviews. In this section, such difficulties in communication are taken for granted. In terms of the model of discourse developed in his work, it has become clear that the voices of the lifeworld and of medicine differ not only in their respective forms of expression, but represent markedly different frameworks of assumptions with different logical properties and domains of reference. Given these differences, an important question for further analysis is how adequate communication and understanding may be achieved.

The task faced by physicians and patients is that they must establish a domain of shared meanings in order to talk with and understand each other. Of course, in most instances, they already share the natural everyday language of their common culture; they are adult speakers who are communicatively competent. Shuy (1974) points out that this assumption may not hold if patients and physicians come from different subcultures or social classes; in his report of interviews between lower class Black patients and middle class white physicians, there is evidence of much misunderstanding and distortion. In the sample of taped interviews used in the present study, all patients and speakers appear to be native speakers of English, thus they can and do rely on their mutual understanding of contextually-grounded referential meanings. Nonetheless, this is not sufficient for what they must accomplish together in the medical interview. The central reason for this is that the framework and range of referential meaning carried by the voice of medicine—the concepts, terms, and logic of medicine as an applied bioscience—represent a technical and specialized language that is clearly and markedly distinguished from the everyday language of the lifeworld.

Another point worth noting is that the availability and use by speakers of different linguistic codes or registers is a common feature of modern complex societies. For example, Gumperz (1972) describes how native Norwegian speakers switch back and forth between local dialects and the official standard form of the language as a function of setting, topic, and other speakers. Bernstein (1971) distinguishes between restricted and elaborated codes and suggests that children lacking competence in the elaborated code used by teachers may not be able to perform adequately in schools. Work on code-switching is germane to problems in the medical interview. Native speakers are usually fluent in several codes and have little difficulty switching from one to the other; the interactional problem turns on their understanding of cues that make one or another code appropriate. However, if a particular code is not in a speaker's repertoire and is required for adequate and acceptable performance—a situation faced by working class and ethnic minority children in elementary schools, as well as by patients in medical settings—then the individual may "fail" to understand and be understood.

The special asymmetry of the medical interview is that physicians are communicatively competent in both codes. They can speak in either the voice of the lifeworld or of medicine, but patients are competent only in one (Hymes, 1971). For this reason, the burden of translating falls primarily on physicians. For communication to produce mutual understanding, physicians must provide equivalences in meaning between statements in one voice and the other and explain differences between alternative contexts. In other words, physicians must translate patients' lifeworld statements into medical terms and medical statements of problems into patients' terms.

The examples given earlier, in analyses of Textual and Interpersonal functions, have already indicated how the physician moves between the two voices and attempts to translate from one to the other. His use of patient terms, such as "weak spells," and his explanation of why it is important for her to know the names of her medications illustrate efforts to make sense in ways that the patient will understand. More significant than particular instances is the way in which he develops and structures the interview so that his diagnosis of anemia as the reason for her "dizziness" and "weak spells" is elaborated and tied to specific diagnostic procedures and lines of questioning. At each step he tries to provide a coherent and meaningful explanation, one that relates her medical history and current symptoms to each other and to the treatment approach he will propose.

About midway through the initial medical history section of the interview, he first states his tentative diagnosis of anemia. He introduces this, as we saw in an exchange presented earlier, by reporting information from her chart:

> Let me tell you one thing that they did draw blood here (P: Ye:s) and I notice that you are anemic. Your chromatica is thirty one .. which is:s .. about . nine or ten points lower than it should be- [P: Hm hm Would that cause (...)] and I dare say that alone would make me feel a little dizzy.

When he offers his diagnosis, he frames it within the formulation of a problem they should work on together and makes explicit the aims of treatment:

> I- I think .... the reason for your weakness and dizziness most likely is gonna turn out that- .. that your . anemia can account for this and what ... I think we should do .. is to find out why you're anemic [P: Huh huh] and what's .... happening to make you have low blood all of a sudden. (P: Hm hm) So that uh .. we can fix ya up .. [P: Hm hm] cause I think ya . still- you still look pretty healthy.

This diagnostic section is itself foreshadowed in the interview when the patient reports that her local physician prescribed pills for high blood pressure; the continued worsening of her "weak spells" then led her to seek other medical help at the clinic. This is followed by the series of exchanges in Transcript 5.5.

In this excerpt, the physician attends to the patient's account of her earlier medical examination. A structure of meaning develops that is in marked contrast to the one underlying and expressed in the voice of medicine. Rather than the abstract and schematized list of questions on unrelated topics with the resulting fragmentation of meaning that we found in analyses of typical interviews, a network of meaningful relations is established. This physician's questions focus on and explore the patient's experiences: "He didn't take any blood from you or do any tests or anything like that," "Did you say that to him?" and "Did he ever give you any pills for anemia?" This last question links back to an earlier patient comment that her physician had said she was a

Transcript 5.5

W:11.110/01

---

001 D He didn't take any blood from you or do any tests or
002   anything like that.
            [
003 P   He did nothing.
004 D   Ungh Okay.
005 P   ....
006 P .... A- A long long ago about a *year* ago I think
007   ...... he said I was a little bit anemic.
008 D   Hm hm
009 P   And at that
010   time I had this sorta a little weak feeling but not . so bad
                                   [
011 D   Yea:h.
012 P .. and so when I was beginning to have these I thought it
013   might be that.
014 D And he didn't- Did you say that to him?
                [
015 P   (...)   He- Yes I said it to
016   him and he took blood from my finger but this was quite a
017   long long ago .... and he said everything was fine ......
018   (...) was .. ya know ...... I dunnow.
019 D   .... Did . he ever
020   give you any pills for the anemia?
021 P   No he told me to take er:r
022   .... vidamins an try that .
023 D   ....
024   .... Okay.

"little bit anemic." Later in the interview he will tie this information to his line of interpretation, diagnosis, and to his plans for further investigation and treatment. The patient's report of her experience remains central not only as the focus of attention, but as the primary point of reference.

In this interview, the two speakers appear to understand each other. Meaning is jointly constructed and shared, and develops in an organic way through their talk. The process is so reasonable and natural that we may forget that these qualities are not found in typical medical interviews, where shared meanings and mutual understandings are not particularly evident. These interviews tend to be marked by disruptions of meanings, by breakdowns in communication, and by the suppression of lifeworld understandings. Examples of such interviews will help to put this into perspective.

Paget (1983a) examines in detail another set of interviews in which misunderstandings and distortions are pervasive. She points out that a principal source of distortion is the physician's active and purposive effort to exclude from the discourse the most significant fact of this patient's medical history. She is a postoperative cancer patient who had a nephrectomy operation about 6 months prior to the interview. The physician is well aware of her history and refers to her diagnostic status in a post-interview questionnaire as "status postnephrectomy for hypernephroma." Nonetheless, over the course of three extended and successive interviews, spaced about a month apart, he never uses the word cancer or explores the relationship of her history with this illness to her current symptoms and complaints.

His references to her experience as a person with a serious life-threatening illness are oblique and couched in euphemisms. He does not refer to her having had an operation for cancer, but makes a vague reference to her "surgery" and the resultant scar. He attempts to reassure her by stating that her one remaining kidney is functionally adequate and that he does not find evidence of a new tumor to account for her symptoms, but he never mentions cancer. Nonetheless, Paget asserts: "Each knew that she had cancer, and each knew that the other knew, and each knew what these oblique references were references to, and, in the ongoing course of their talk, each also knew that these oblique references were recurring without achieving expression" (pp. 15-16). The suppressed topic "hovers" in the background but is lost in the discourse. It is concealed by the physician's treating each complaint as if it is discrete and unrelated to the others, and he continues to reassure her that her basic health is good.

Within this discourse, permeated by evasion, concealment, and distortion, the physician presses an interpretation that involves a radical transformation of meaning. He attributes her problems to "nerves," to her emotional and psychological difficulties, and in various ways urges her to consider psychiatric treatment. Early in the interview, he foreshadows the direction his interpretation will take by his response to the patient's anguished plea for explanation and help; she is feeling the terrible strain of having "so darned many complaints," without adequate diagnosis or effective treatment. He says, "There has to be some explanation but it d- (noise) .... b- it doesn't haftuh be:: A dise:ase in order t' organize-."[4] The implication that there may be nonmedical reasons for her problem is initiated later, when he abruptly asks: "D' y' have any problems in yer home, with your husband or is that-" and "Do y' think you were having more than average problems or probably less." Finally, he asks more explicitly, "Well has it possibly occurred to you that with all the troubles that yer .... body has gone through, that yer nerves have now got to the point where they suffer, an' where you need help to get yer nerves restored" (the extra stress they each place on specific words is marked here by underlining).

She resists his interpretation: "I jus'- there's a reason for my not feelin' this: good n' I don't think it's nerves." He does not explore her feelings, but counters her resistance: "Well y' may y' may have to explore a different possibilities .... Because I hope you don't think the doctors er holding out on you." At the end of the third interview, he is still reassuring her that her health is good and that the problem is her nerves. But the patient's last statement is: "If I have a stomach ache that bu:rns I feel tha- that's nerves but these pains are definite pains (D: W'l we'll have to wait a see.) The- the pains are definite pa:ins and I really don't uh attribute them to nerves."

When physicians are oblique rather than direct in their comments, and use euphemisms to refer to illnesses and treatments, they may confuse and frighten patients. Patients have to take the initiative in order to arrive at an adequate understanding of what is being said and done. This physician, who persists in using the vague term "nerves," also avoids explicitly stating the obvious recommendation for this problem and forces it to come from the patient. He remarks that since neither he nor other physicians have been able to find a medical basis for her problems, she should

---

[4] Physician and patient utterances quoted here are taken from Paget's transcription of this interview.

explore other "possibilities." He says: "I::: think sooner or later if these things go on yer gonna haf to explore .... y:e:r the problem of yer nerves: ..... becuz whether it's primary or secondary it's what's holding you up." After this comment, it is the patient who finally says: "Uh huh .... Psychiatry." Even after she has used the word, he tries to avoid saying it himself.

A similar pattern of evasion and attendant lack of clarity is found in another interview, W:12.118/02. The patient is a young woman whose breasts have not developed; various tests have not revealed any hormonal abnormalities and the physician is suggesting possible next steps. He mentions hormonal therapy and then refers to surgery in the following way: "If that doesn't work there really aren't any other things to do other than the plastics that he- that he brought up." He repeats this later in the same utterance, but just as obliquely: "to try the hormonal therapy if that's not successful then uh just be up to you as to whether you uh want to go any further .... and I can get uh ya know get in touch uh uh the surgeons .... if you're so inclined." All of this leaves the patient somewhat confused and she asks: "So is there an alternative of hormonal therapy still?" Finally, he refers to plastic surgery as something she might "obviously want to think about after we try this." He suggests that she call him in a few months if she's inclined to "pursue it further" and he will find out "the best way to go- to go about getting you seen by the surgeons to get their opinions et cetera." In all his statements he never explicitly refers to breast surgery. Despite the obvious affective meaning of the problem to the patient, he has assiduously avoided it, and concludes with another euphemism: "Basically we're after a cosmetic effect anyway."

The vagueness of reference and the indirection of the talk just cited is not unusual in typical medical interviews. Findings from other studies show that withholding and concealment of information, and physicians' evasion of patient requests resulting in uncertainty and confusion, is widespread (Hauser, 1981). For that reason, the interview we have been examining in this chapter offers a striking contrast. As this physician pursues his investigation, he provides information and the reasons for each procedure. He appears to recognize that the patient may not understand the relevance of certain procedures and tests; thus, in the following excerpt (Transcript 5.6), he explains why he wants to do a rectal examination.

Transcript 5.6

W:11.110/01

```
001 D  Okay. Good. Wy don't you ........ get into a jo:hnny if you
002    could?
003 P          Hm hm
                 [
004 D                 And uh .... we'll examine you. I'm gonna want to
005    do a rectal exam.
006 P                  Hm hm
007 D                          Check your s- stool to see if you do
008    have any blood there. .. Uh The fact that you are anemic
009    ...... uh:h ........ is of some concern to me in terms of why
010    you should be anemic .... uh whether the pills you've been
011    taking uh have anything to do with it I don't know.
012 P                                        I haven't
013    been takin the pills.
                 [
014 D        Uh:h         You have- . Maybe not. You have other
                             [               [
015 P                        Heh heh        Heh heh
016 D reasons to be anemic. You have what's known as diverticulosis
                       [
017 P                  Oh:m
018 D ............ uh little- . little outpouchings on your . large
019    intestine.
020 P          Oh I see.
021 D                          And this sometimes can cause some bleeding.
022 D .... uh People with . hi- hiatus hernias up here sometimes
                                                    [
023 P                                               Hm:m
024 D can have some bleeding. ........ And uh ................
025    something that we can fix and we want to check on to make sure.
                                                    [
026 P                                               Uhm hm
```

He is direct and concrete in his explanation of the possibility that her anemia may be a result of bleeding from a hiatus hernia, a problem she has previously mentioned, or from diverticulosis, a technical term that he quickly translates. Later, after completing the rectal examination, he reports the results and brings the subplot in this story to a resolved ending. He then links it to the next steps to be taken:

> Your stool that I sampled was negative .. so there's no blood in it
> .... ah:h but it- but you are .... anemic .... so that we ..
> have to .. pursue some sort of an investigation [P: Hm:hm] right
> now in terms of why you are anemic. .... So . let me .
> just talk with you ask you a few questions to begin with about that.
> ...... You- You cook for yourself?

After a detailed review of her diet and eating habits, as well as of her pattern of activity and involvement with her children, he moves toward termination of the interview. In Transcript 5.7, he ties together the various strands of the interview. The central theme he has developed is repeated in concrete and explicit terms: the task is to find reasons for her anemia and implement a treatment program that will help to "build your blood back up again." A new proposal, to stop her blood pressure pills "for now," is connected to his overall impression and plan. His reassurance, "I think basically you're still in pretty good health," does not have the ad hoc and mechanical quality that we often find in other interviews but fits meaningfully into the understanding of her problems that has developed over the course of their talking together.

Discussion. By examining ways in which referential meaning is developed and sustained, the interpenetration of the three functions of discourse has become particularly evident. The Textual, Interpersonal, and Ideational functions are analytically distinct. Nonetheless, they are all omnipresent and achieved simultaneously through the concrete particulars of speech. It is impossible to conceive of discourse that is cohesive but has no content or defined relationships between speakers, nor can either of the latter stand by themselves.

On the other hand, these functions are independent of each other in the strict sense that the features of language through which

Transcript 5.7

W:11.110/01

```
001  D  Okay. Fine. Well . what we're gonna do is I'll- I'm gonna
002     ...... order some uh uh blood studies on you.
003  P                                          Hm hm
004  D                                                  And uh ..
005     we'll see ............ uh what we can do in terms of trying
006     to find out why you're anemic and what we can do to build
007     your blood back up again ...... and uh .. what I'd like you
008     also to do is to stop these blood pressure pills for now.
                                        [
009  P                                          Hm:m
010  P  Yea:h. Well see I don't take em (...)-
                [
011  D           Next time I see you we'll *see* what your blood pressure
012     is:s.
            [
013  P  (...) Yea:h.
014  D              ........ And I'd like to- .......... These are
                            [
015  P                 Hm:m
016  D  fairly *stro*ng pills.
017  P                 Yeah I would think so.
018  D                                      An uh I'd like
019     to give you something that's- *if* you *nee*d it. I don't kno:w.
020     When you get your blood- your .............. blood built
021     back up again you may not need it .... uh and we can start
                                        [
022  P                                          Hm:m
023  D  you on something that's a little milder and uh ..........
024     not near- not nearly as strong as these are. ........ Jus-
            [
025  P     Hm:m
026  D  Have to go *slo*wly I think as long as you're doing *ver*y well
027     now . we'll uh go slow and we'll do it correctly and get
```

```
028       to the root of this ............ Have you back feelin good
029       in no time at all. I think basically you're still in
                              [
030   P                      Heh Heh
031   D   pretty good health.
```

they are realized, the options available, and the systematic connections among them, are different from each other. For that reason, we look to different aspects of talk when we try to understand how a particular type of cohesion is accomplished than when we try to understand the development of shared meanings between speakers. Theoretically, the autonomy of the functions and their respective ways of realization would imply the possibility of empirical independence. In other words, any type of cohesion might be associated with any type of speaker relationship and meaning construction. Thought experiments, if not real experiments, might be designed to test and demonstrate this possibility.

Analyses presented in this and previous sections strongly suggest that the theoretical independence of these different functions is not found in practice. Instead, it appears that there is an empirical concordance among the ways in which cohesion is produced, the type of relationship developed between speakers, and the process through which speakers arrive at shared meanings.

Specifically, in the interview selected for analysis, the physician attempts to bring the patient with him as he increases his understanding of her problems and develops a treatment plan. A particularly significant characteristic of his mode of participation is that he listens to the patient's accounts with minimum interruption. This deserves special emphasis since the act of listening is inaudible on the tape recording and invisible on the printed transcript. Nevertheless, listening is as much a part of discourse as speaking.

Again, contrast with more typical medical interviews underscores the different quality of this one. Listening is a necessary condition for the joint construction of meanings, but it is not sufficient. The listener must show that she/he has been paying attention, not simply waiting to take her/his turn. This physician ties his questions and comments to the patient's accounts. In this way, he shows that he has not only listened, but that he has heard.

He refers explicitly to what she has said, explains how his evaluation and recommendations are related to what she has told him, and reformulates his impressions at various points to include new information that she provides. Earlier I referred to this process as organic. This quality exists in large part because the physician's formulations respect the integrity of the patient's story. His technical understanding is translated and incorporated into the structure of meanings expressed in the voice of the lifeworld. This is the reverse of what we found in typical medical interviews in which the lifeworld was "absorbed" into the technocratic consciousness expressed in the voice of medicine.

Constructing a discourse of shared meanings, by overcoming the problem of incompatible voices without coerciveness, is related intimately to both the type of cohesion and form of relationship established in this interview. This is the empirical concordance I alluded to earlier. For example, the physician's use of open-ended questions and transitional comments provides a different type of cohesiveness than that found in typical interviews organized by physicians' closed-ended questions and abrupt transitions. But these cohesion-producing devices also serve to generate a discourse of shared meanings that reflects the physician's attentiveness and responsiveness to the patient. We also found that his apparent departures from "normatively-governed" ways of relating to the patient consisted in this responsiveness to her particular circumstances and life contexts. Thus, his ways of relating to her parallel and intersect with how he makes sense, in collaboration with the patient, of what is wrong and what can be done.

Once again, the point must be made, that although this interview is in striking contrast to others we have examined it is clearly an example of a medical interview. For that reason, it is a concrete demonstration of the possibility of more responsive and humane clinical practice.

Conclusion: Attending to the Voice of the Lifeworld

In this chapter, I addressed one central question: What are the characteristics of a medical interview in which the physician is relatively more attentive to the voice of the lifeworld than usual in typical interviews? Two closely related questions were also addressed: How do the two types of interview differ from each other? How do these differences bear on our interpretation of clinical practice, particularly with regard to essential differences and conflict between the voices of the lifeworld and of medicine?

As in earlier stages in this investigation, analyses of attentiveness both extend previous findings and, at the same time, revise them. I referred to this approach as the research strategy of "interruption." There were several ways in which this strategy was carried out. First, in analyses of "unremarkable" interviews and then of interviews in which the voice of the lifeworld interrupted the voice of medicine, I focused on typical interviews; the features of such interviews were interpreted as reflecting the organization of standard clinical practice. In this chapter, I searched for an "atypical" interview, one in which the disjunction between voices and the attendant dissonance was muted and in which the timbre of the discourse had a different quality.

Second, I reversed the direction of the analysis. In earlier analyses, I proceeded somewhat inductively. I moved from description to interpretation to interruption, beginning with specific features of the discourse and, on that basis, developed the concepts of the structure of the standard medical interview and of the two voices. For example, evidence of disruptions in the fluency of physician's speech led to the interpretation of conflict between the different voices. Here, I have proceeded more deductively, beginning with an interview that appeared "atypical" in its overall quality and then examining it for specific, distinctive features.

Finally, and also deductively, I borrowed and applied a framework for analysis that represented a general theory of language rather than one representing the particular type of language under study, the discourse of medical interviews. This was done in a heuristic, rather than systematic, fashion. Halliday's model of discourse functions is sufficiently comprehensive to permit the detailed comparison of different types of interviews in terms of specific features of discourse. The approach proved useful. I was able to show in some detail how this atypical interview was constructed, and how ways of achieving textual cohesion, speaker relationships, and referential meaning differed from those found in more typical interviews.

Nonetheless, despite the results, I must return to a caveat noted at the beginning of the chapter. The analysis has been limited to an instance I was fortunate to find in a corpus of medical interviews drawn from standard clinical practice. These instances are rare. More significantly, such atypical interviews are unlikely to represent types of physician attentiveness to patients that might be found in clinical situations reflecting a more radical restructuring of medicine and patient care. Contextual considerations are of critical importance in interpreting these findings. More specifically, it is within the context of ordinary practice, dominated by the voice of medicine, that this particular physician's ways of speech stand out in striking fashion. A physician who listens, asks open-ended questions, and translates his technical understanding into the language of the lifeworld contrasts sharply with other physicians. The contrast has been central to these analyses. I am now pointing out that the discourse features selected for comparison reflect our prior understanding of typical practice. Thus, the full meaning of this physician's atypicality must be understood with reference to the pattern of discourse found in ordinary practice with the latter serving as the context used to interpret this interview. In the context of other, perhaps more radical forms of practice, these same discourse features might have quite a different meaning.

There is an additional caveat about the interpretation of these findings. It is important to make a distinction between attentiveness to the voice of the lifeworld and two other modes of physician response to patients that bear a superficial similarity to it. The first is the approach of psychiatrically-oriented physicians concerned with the affective, psychological, and symbolic meanings of patients' accounts. In interviews I have examined, recommendations to patients that they seek psychiatric help, or diagnoses suggesting that the "real" problem is nerves or psychological stress or anxiety, do not reflect attentiveness in my sense of it. Rather than opening up a mutual discussion of patients' problems, the "psychiatric" approach is used by physicians in ways that appear to extend the biomedical model to a nonmedical domain of issues. It often marks a lack of attentiveness to patients' lifeworlds and to experientially-grounded understandings of their problems. The interview excerpts presented in this chapter as contrasting examples, in which the physician persists in a diagnosis of "nerves" against the patient's resistance, well illustrate this pattern of inattentiveness to the patient's lifeworld within a psychiatric perspective.

I am not suggesting, of course, that insensitivity to psychological aspects of patients' medical problems is a sign of good humane practice. However, I am asserting that the lifeworld of patients is not equivalent to or captured within the worldview of psychiatry. The latter has a particular technical perspective which is a subvariant of the more general biomedical model. Whether it enters into the discourse between patients and physicians within a context of attentiveness to the lifeworld or whether it enters only as a special dialect of the dominant voice of medicine is a question that must be, and can only be, tested in each particular instance.

The "friendly" physician is another type that must be distinguished from the attentive one. Berger (1969) points out that the doctor is a "witness" to patients' suffering and pain and offers "fraternity," the function of which is "recognition."

> It would be a great mistake to "normalize" what I have just said by concluding that quite naturally the patient wants a *friendly* doctor. His hopes and demands ... are much more profound and precise. In illness many connexions are severed. Illness separates and encourages a distorted, fragmented form of self-consciousness. The doctor, through his relationship with the invalid and by means of the special intimacy he is allowed, has to compensate for these broken connections and reaffirm the social content of the individual's aggravated self-consciousness. (pp. 68-69)

Berger's term "recognition" corresponds to the meaning of attentiveness as I have used it. His comment on the qualities of a "good doctor" will bring to a close my exploration of the ways in which attentiveness to the lifeworlds of patients permits physicians to retrieve the possibility of humane care within the context and conditions of ordinary clinical practice.

> ... he is acknowledged as a good doctor because he meets the deep but unformulated expectation of the sick for a sense of fraternity. He recognizes them. ... there is about him the constant will of a man trying to recognize. ... It is as though when he talks or listens to a patient, he is also touching them with his hands so as to be less likely to misunderstand: and it is as though, when he is physically examining the patient, they were also conversing. (pp. 76-77)

CHAPTER 6

Observations on Humane Practice and Critical Research

The study of medical interviews reported in the preceding chapters embodies a general perspective about both clinical practice and research. The specific features and implications of this perspective emerged gradually over the course of the work. In a reciprocal and dialectical way, it was shaped by problems encountered and solutions adopted at successive stages of investigation and, in turn, the study was shaped by this perspective as it developed. Its essential and primary components are expressed in capsule form in the title of this concluding chapter: humane practice and critical research. Though embedded within successive analyses and interpretations, the meaning and significance of these particular forms of research and practice have remained implicit. The task undertaken in the following pages is to explicate these two terms and to explore the relationships between them.

The discussion is framed and guided by the status of these terms as idealizations. They assert certain values that would ideally inform the direction and aims of practice and research. Reference to them helps us to assess the degree and ways in which particular instances correspond or deviate from these ideals. This assessment suggests topics and directions for further work. Thus, it is evident that various limitations and inadequacies of the present study preclude any claim that a full understanding of humane practice has been achieved or that this is an exemplar of critical research. It was difficult, for example, to find clear instances of medical interviews in which the lifeworld contexts of patients' problems were the principal source for the structuring of discourse and the construction of meaning. For that reason, analysis of the type of practice that was central to our concerns was restricted to an interview that only partially represented the ideal; one in which the physician was relatively more attentive to the voice of the lifeworld. This limits what may be said about the various forms and features of humane practices.

Similarly, the methods used for the analysis of discourse, the research strategy of interruption analysis, and the conceptual approach to interpretation do not adequately represent critical research.[1] This term, introduced for the first time now, is intended to refer to an approach that includes several distinctive components, each only partially realized in this study: critical reflection on assumptions and methods of research, commitment to the values of humane clinical practice, and methods of research appropriate to the object of study and consistent with the aims and features of humane practice.

These brief definitions will be developed more fully in the following discussion. Despite the limitations of this study, the statement of these aims as idealizations provides a context for reviewing the work and exploring its implications. The view that practice and research are interdependent will be a central theme in this discussion. In particular, I hope to show that a critical approach to research can contribute to the understanding and development of humane practice.

The two aims have different histories. The research strategy of interruption analysis developed within the ongoing conduct of the study. Further, it is only now when reflecting back on the

---

[1] The term critical research was chosen to make explicit an affinity between this approach and "critical theory," a theoretical perspective associated primarily with the Frankfurt school of sociology. Critical research may be viewed as a specific application of Habermas' formulation of emancipatory science; his analysis has been a critical resource for the development of this approach to research. An informative history of the Frankfurt school and its approach is found in Jay (1973). A perceptive analysis of critical theory may be found in Bernstein (1978). Some of the significant contrasts between critical theory and the positivist model of science are discussed in Adorno et al. (1976). The idea of emancipatory science is developed in Habermas (1971, 1973). Finally, an excellent introduction to the full range of Habermas' work is found in McCarthy (1978).

work that it is identified as a specification of critical research. In contrast, the study began with the aim of studying humane medical care as it might be expressed in patient-physician discourse. The initial definition of humane care in the study proposal was specified and elaborated as the study proceeded, but is clear that the early formulation of humane care was retained:

> ... the acknowledgement and response to patients' presenting problems in terms of the "meanings" of these problems in patients' lifeworlds. This may be contrasted to a response framed solely within a biomedical framework where signs and symptoms are used to classify a patient as a "case," that is, as someone with a disease. (Mishler, 1979, p. 3)

As the study progressed through successive stages of analysis, this formulation was specified as a distinction between the voice of the lifeworld and the voice of medicine. These voices were found to represent different frameworks of logic and meaning expressed in the talk of patients and physicians. Analyses revealed, in detail, the ways in which discourse was shaped by the interaction between the two voices.

The conception of voices, and their description and interpretation in terms of functions of specific features of discourse, depended upon the development and application of an innovative research strategy. This new approach developed as the work proceeded. The design and proposed methods of study were initially framed within the mainstream tradition of research. However, the limitations of this approach became apparent as problems in attempting to provide adequate and appropriate descriptions, analyses, and interpretations of the discourse of medical interviews were encountered. This led to a critique of traditional methods using two essential components.

First, I tried to demonstrate the inappropriateness of traditional methods that laid a claim on objectivity and placed a premium on standardization for the study of organized and meaningful discourse. The principal reason for their failure was that they stripped away social contexts of meaning, and the inclusion of these contexts in analyses was a prerequisite to an understanding of discourse. Second, I argued that past studies of medical interviews, with rare exceptions, relied implicitly on assumptions of the biomedical model. Interpretations of findings were constrained and informed by these assumptions and, therefore, reflected a medical bias, that is, the meaning and significance of various features of the discourse was understood and explained by investigators from the perspective of physicians.

The new research strategy was not based on this critique, but rather developed hand-in-hand with it. The task was to devise methods that were more appropriate to the study of discourse and, at the same time, did not adopt a medical bias as the basis for understanding issues of humane care. The research strategy implemented, termed "interruption analysis," relied, as a first step, on the critical questioning of assumptions underlying traditional methods of description and analysis and a parallel questioning of biomedical assumptions that entered into interpretations of findings. As a second step, along with the application of alternative methods of description and analysis, there was a shift in the focus of inquiry. The voice of the lifeworld and patients' accounts of their problems became the central topics.

The new approach led to a radical reinterpretation of the structure and functions of clinical discourse. Initial analyses of "unremarkable" interviews, that relied implicitly on a medical bias, produced a picture of orderly and coherent discourse, marred by occasional patient disruptions, but essentially under the firm control of physicians speaking in the voice of medicine. Interrupting these analyses led to a different understanding, at levels of both description and interpretation. From the new perspective, with the voice of the lifeworld at the center of interest, medical interviews were found to be arenas of struggle, marked and shaped by conflict between the voices of the lifeworld and of medicine. Typically, the voice of the lifeworld was suppressed and patients' efforts to provide accounts of their problems within the contexts of their lifeworld situations were disrupted and fragmented. The apparent orderly surface of a typical medical interview, revealed in the first series of analyses, was deceptive and obscured its "disorderliness" at a deeper level.

Finally, in order to demonstrate the possibility of an alternative mode of clinical practice, an interview was examined in which a physician displayed an atypical degree of attentiveness to the voice of the lifeworld. This discourse was qualitatively different in many respects from typical interviews as the latter lacked some degree of reciprocity between the voices and were dominated by the voice of medicine.

This spare description of both major turning points in the research and of the principal line of reasoning developed serves to bring forward certain issues that up to now have remained in the background. Clearly, in addition to reporting a specific study of medical interviews, this book is a general critique of current forms of both clinical practice and research. The evaluative stance embedded and reflected in this critique is expressed in the statement of ideal aims with which this chapter began. The following observations, focused on the implications of the study, are framed and informed by these aims.

An essential assumption of this work is the importance of humane care as a criterion for assessing clinical practice. Although it was undoubtedly evident to the reader, this assumption was not explicitly justified. Rather, general agreement on the necessity for humane care was presupposed. In a loose sense, this presupposition was probably true—one would not expect any particular practitioner or investigator to be opposed to humane care. However, an alternative criterion, about which this text is silent, is more prominent in discussions and studies of health care. This is the criterion of effectiveness, expressed in such questions as: "Do patients get better?" "Are diseases and illnesses cured?" and "Do the treatments result in reductions in rates of morbidity and mortality?"

These are not trivial questions and their neglect in this study is not intended to belie their importance. However, a serious problem arises when these two criteria, humaneness and effectiveness, are placed in opposition. The view that these criteria are not only different, but opposed to each other, is not unusual. In class discussions of physician-patient relationships, for example, medical students have reported that they are sometimes confronted by their teachers with the question: "Do you want to be a nice guy or a good doctor?" I take the view that this is a specious question. It identifies humaneness with being "nice," a spurious identification that will be discussed more fully below, and it implies that effectiveness and humaneness are not only independent of each other, but may be contradictory. In contrast, within the perspective on clinical practice that has informed this study, the two aims are consistent with and parallel to each other. Stated more strongly and concisely, humane care is effective care and, to be effective care must be humane.

This assertion is grounded in the specific definition and conceptualization of humane care developed and implemented in this study. Briefly, humane care refers to the primacy accorded to patients' lifeworld contexts of meaning as the basis for understanding, diagnosing, and treating their problems. Within the particular field of medical interviews, humaneness of care, in the sense of the primacy of these contexts, was assessed by the strength of the voice of the lifeworld in shaping the discourse and by the attentiveness of physicians to this voice.

The argument developed through detailed analyses of medical interviews that a discourse dominated by the voice of medicine represents a practice that is not humane is now being extended: such a discourse is also an ineffective practice. The reason is that the voice of medicine relies exclusively on the biomedical model (Mishler, 1981). This model, reflecting the technical-instrumental framework of the biosciences, strips away social contexts of meaning on which a full and adequate understanding of patients and their illnesses depend. Effectiveness of practice depends on such an understanding. Thus, to bring this argument to a close, humaneness and effectiveness of care are bound together and do not stand in opposition to each other.

In an earlier chapter, this view of humane care is distinguished from two other conceptions that are apparently similar. These are expressed, respectively, as recommendations that physicians adopt a more "friendly" attitude towards their patients and that they develop an awareness of the psychiatric or psychological components of patients' illnesses. Friendliness and an increased sensitivity to psychological dynamics may have a number of benefits for improving the quality of patient-physician relationships, but neither is a sufficient condition for humane care.

Friendly or "nice" physicians may still function exclusively within a biomedical framework and speak in a register restricted to the voice of medicine, even though the voice has undertones of positive feeling. Similarly, a psychiatric orientation can merely reflect the extension of the biomedical perspective into the domains of thought and affect rather than a transformation of understanding that includes the lifeworld contexts of patients' problems. Attentiveness to the voice of the lifeworld is neither friendship nor psychiatry. Berger's (1969) term "recognition" comes closer to the intended meaning of humane care. Recognition of the distinctive humanity of patients and respect for the contextual grounding of their problems in their lifeworlds is the essential ingredient.

From this discussion it is clear that strengthening the voice of the lifeworld promotes both humaneness and effectiveness of care. The critical question is: How can the voice of the lifeworld be strengthened? Answers to this question depend on an analysis of the forces and conditions that may either weaken or strengthen this voice within the larger context of the health care system and, more broadly still, the sociocultural, economic, and political context in which the system functions. Such an analysis is beyond the boundaries of this book. However, one significant and pervasive feature of the system may be singled out for brief comment since it represents a problem that is central for both analyses and proposals for change in the health care system. This is the problem of power.

Current forms of clinical practice are based on and incorporate an asymmetric power relationship between patients and health care workers. Medical interviews display this asymmetry as demonstrated in this study. The relationship between humane care and differentials in power may be seen by reformulating the earlier question on how to strengthen the voice of the lifeworld to: How can patients be empowered? This shifts the focus, but does not change the deep meaning of the question. Achieving humane care is dependent upon empowering patients.

Why are these equivalencies important for research? If practice and research are interdependent, what is the direction and form of research that would be relevant to and support the aim of humane practice? A general approach, referred to here as critical research, is proposed as a framework for investigation. In critical research, the equivalencies between humane practice, the primacy of the lifeworld, the effectiveness of care, and the empowerment of patients are central topics of inquiry.

Among the questions to which such research might be directed is the following: What are the specific features of humane care in the various contexts of clinical practice and what are the obstacles to its achievement? Only one type of clinical situation is included in the present study. Although the medical interview is a significant part of health care, there are many other treatment and diagnostic contexts that merit investigation. These include, for example, patterns of hospital care and the management of chronically ill patients in family and community settings; both of these would extend the field of observation to include other health care professionals such as nurses and social workers as well as significant participants in patients' social networks. The extension of inquiry in this direction would require development and refinement of the concept of humane practice which has been particularly specified in this study as the strength of the voice of the lifeworld in the discourse between patients and physicians.

Another line of inquiry could focus on the problem of the effectiveness of treatment. The argument presented earlier that humane practice and effectiveness are interdependent suggests that current criteria are inadequate and that the meaning of effectiveness requires reformulation. Symptom relief, length of hospital stay, compliance with physicians' recommendations, even patient satisfaction with medical care, are insufficient. None of these usual criteria refer to or enlarge our understanding of the critical question of how illnesses and treatments affect the functioning of patients in their lifeworlds. Such an exploration would shift attention away from concerns that are defined and restricted by assumptions of the biomedical model to a social perspective in which patients' relationships and involvements in family, community, and work settings have primary significance.

Finally, relationships between power and practice are important topics for investigation. The dependence, asserted earlier, between humane practice and the empowerment of patients points to a number of specific questions for research. For example, what are the effects of different approaches to the empowerment of patients on clinical practice? How is the discourse of clinical interviews affected by patients' participation in patient advocacy groups? How can institutions of health care be reorganized so that patients can have a stronger voice in decisions about their care and treatment? In what ways can the training and education of physicians and other health care professionals be changed to encourage responsiveness and attentiveness to the voice of the lifeworld?

The discussion to this point has centered on the types of questions that would be addressed by critical research. In contrast to a more traditional or mainstream approach, no claim is made to neutrality. Rather, these questions reflect a commitment to the values of humane care and, more specifically, to the definition of such care in terms of the primacy of lifeworld contexts of meaning. I have also proposed that another essential feature of critical research is the use of methods that are appropriate and in accord with the features and aims of humane practice. In the present study of medical interviews, these criteria were approached by applying methods of description and analysis that preserved the structure and organization of meaning in natural discourse and, via the critique of biomedical assumptions provided by interruption analysis, by placing the voice of the lifeworld at the center of inquiry. However, the issue of the relationship between humane practices and research methods is complex and cannot be resolved by extrapolation to other studies of the methods used here.

A useful way to approach the problem is to note the similarity between the use of technical procedures and methods in research and the use of technical procedures and methods in health care. In neither case is the application of a specific procedure an adequate index of whether or not the practice is or is not humane. Rather, this determination depends on analysis of contexts of use. To restate and extend the argument presented earlier, a practice is less humane to the extent that it is dominated by a technocratic perspective and represents the triumph of the technocratic consciousness.[2] This applies to both research and clinical care. In contrast, to the degree that specific instances of clinical and research practice reflect recognition and respect for patients' lifeworlds and orient interpretation and treatment around the primacy of the lifeworld, they may be viewed as approximating the ideals, respectively, of humane practice and critical research.

It is perhaps too grand to refer to studies as voyages of discovery, but the image has the right resonance. At the least, studies are explorations, forays into unknown territory. Similar to explorers, investigators have several obligations in reporting their observations: to tell what they have found, to interpret its significance, and to point to what is still unknown, to the uncharted areas that require continued exploration and study. In retracing the path taken in this research, describing landmarks along the

---

[2] This view is consistent with the argument developed by Stanley in his critical and perceptive analysis of the "technological conscience." He makes a similar distinction between the tools and methods that constitute a technology and "technicism," or "metaphorical misapplications of some of the assumptions, imagery, and linguistic habits of science and technology to areas of discourse in which such mistakes obscure the free and responsible nature of humane action. As such, technicism is a break in the evolution of linguistic understanding and self-control, a cul-de-sac of mystification" (Stanley 1978, p. xiii).

way as a guide for other investigators, this last chapter has adopted a utopian vision. Humane practice and critical research are the twin poles of this vision. They provide standards for assessing the implications and significance of this study, and of others as well, and stake out directions for future work.

The effort to understand the interdependence between clinical and research practices has revealed that they both, in their current forms, are hampered and restricted by the same assumptions and bias of a technological perspective. Their respective foci of attention are narrowed to fragmented and disjointed bits of human experience and their aims are framed and specified by a tightly-constrained set of technical criteria. In drawing upon a utopian vision, the intent of this chapter has been to initiate and encourage a shift away from the technological perspective to one grounded in lifeworld contexts of meaning. In this way, humaneness may be recovered as the essential criterion for both clinical practice and research.

Bibliography

Adorno, T. W., Albert, H., Dahrendorf, R., Habermas, J., Pilot, H., & Popper, K. R. (1976). *The positivist dispute in German sociology*. New York: Harper and Row.

Bales, R. F. (1950a). *Interaction process analysis*. Reading, MA: Addison-Wesley Press.

Bales, R. F. (1950b). A set of categories for the analysis of small group interaction. *American Sociological Review, 15,* 257–263.

Barrows, H. S. (1968). Simulated patients in medical teaching. *Canadian Medical Association Journal, 98,* 674–76.

Berger, J., & Mohr, J. (1969). *A fortunate man: The story of a country doctor*. Harmondsworth, England: Penguin Books.

Bernstein, B. (1971). *Class, codes and control* (Vol 1). *Theoretical studies toward a sociology of language*. London: Routledge and Kegan Paul.

Bernstein, R. J. (1978). *The restructuring of social and political theory*. Philadelphia, PA: University of Pennsylvania Press.

Blackwell, B. (1973). Drug therapy: Patient compliance. *New England Journal of Medicine, 289,* 249–252.

Bosk, C. L. (1979). *Forgive and remember: Managing medical failure*. Chicago, IL: University of Chicago Press.

Byrne, P. S., Long, B. E. L. (1976). *Doctors talking to patients*. London: HMSO.

Cairns, R.B. (Ed.). (1979). *The analysis of social interactions: Methods, issues, and illustrations*. Hillsdale, NJ: Lawrence Erlbaum Associates.

Cairns, R. B. (1979). Toward guidelines for interactional research. In R. B. Cairns (Ed.), *The analysis of social interactions: Methods, issues, and illustrations.* Hillsdale, NJ: Lawrence Erlbaum Associates.

Carini, P. F. (1975). *Observation and description: An alternative methodology for the investigation of human phenomena* (Monograph of the North Dakota Study Group on Evaluation). Grand Forks, ND: University of North Dakota Press.

Cohen, J. (1960). A coefficient of agreement for nominal scales. *Journal of Educational and Psychological Measurement, 20,* 37–46.

Coulthard, M., & Ashby, M. (1975). Talking with the doctor, 1. *Journal of Communication, 25*(3), 140–48.

Davis, M. (1968). Variations in patients' compliance with doctors' advice: An empirical analysis of patterns of communication. *American Journal of Public Health, 58*(2), 274–288.

Duff, R., & Hollingshead, A. B. (1968). *Sickness and society.* New York: Harper & Row.

Dunbar, J., & Stunkard, A. (1979). Adherence to diet and drug regimen. In R. Levy, B. Rifkind, B. Dennis, & N. Ernst (Eds.), *Nutrition, lipids, and coronary heart disease.* New York: Raven Press.

Ehrenreich, B., & Ehrenreich, J. (1971). *The American health empire: Power, profits, and politics.* New York: Vintage Books.

Emerson, J. P. (1970). Behavior in private places: Sustaining definitions of reality in gynecological examinations. In H. P. Dreitzel (Ed.), *Recent Sociology* (Vol. 2). New York: Macmillan.

Filmer, P., Phillipson, M., Silverman, D., & Walsh, D. (1972). *New directions in sociological theory.* Cambridge, MA: MIT Press.

Fisher, S., & Todd, A. D. (1983). *The social organization of doctor-patient communication.* Washington, DC: Center for Applied Linguistics.

Francis, V., Korsch, B. M., & Morris, M. J. (1969). Gaps in doctor-patient communication: Patients' response to medical advice. *New England Journal of Medicine, 280*(10), 535–540.

Frankel, R. M. (1983). The laying on of hands: Aspects of the organization of gaze, touch, and talk in a medical encounter. In S. Fisher & A. D. Todd (Eds.), *The social organization of doctor-patient communication.* Washington, DC: Center for Applied Linguistics.

Frankel, R. M. (Ed.). (1984). Physicians and patients in social interaction: Medical encounters as a discourse process. *Discourse Processes,* Special Issue, 7, 103–224.

Frankel, R. M. (in press). Talking in interviews: A dispreference for patient initiated questions in physician-patient encounters. In G. Psathas (Ed.), *Interaction competence.* New York: Irvington Publishers.

Freemon, B., Negrete, V. F., Davis, M., & Korsch, B. M. (1971). Gaps in doctor-patient communication: Doctor-patient interaction analysis. *Pediatric Research, 5,* 298–311.

Freire, P. (1968). *Pedagogy of the oppressed.* New York: Herder and Herder.

Fries, C. C. (1965). *English word lists: A study of their adaptability for instruction.* Ann Arbor, MI: George Wahr Publishing Co.

Gallagher, E. B. (1978). *The doctor-patient relationship in the changing health scene.* DHEW Publication No. (NIH) 78–183. Washington, DC: USGPO.

Garfinkel, H. (1967). *Studies in ethnomethodology.* Englewood Cliffs, NJ: Prentice-Hall.

Garfinkel, H. (1976). *An introduction, for novices, to the work of studying naturally organized ordinary activities.* Unpublished Manuscript.

Garfinkel, H., Lynch, M., & Livingston, E. (1980, October). *The work of a discovering science construed with materials from the optically discovered pulsar.* Paper presented at the meeting for Science and Technology Studies, Toronto, Canada.

Garfinkel, H., & Sacks, H. (1970). On formal structures and practical actions. In J. C. McKinney & E. A. Tiryakian (Eds.), *Theoretical sociology: Perspectives and development.* New York: Appleton-Century-Crofts.

Gumperz, J. J. (1972). Social meaning in linguistic structures: Code-switching in Norway. In J. J. Gumperz & D. Hymes (Eds.), *Directions in sociolinguistics: The ethnography of communication.* New York: Holt, Rinehart and Winston.

Habermas, J. (1970). *Toward a rational society.* Boston, MA: Beacon Press.

Habermas, J. (1971). *Knowledge and human interests.* Boston, MA: Beacon Press.

Habermas, J. (1973). A postscript to *Knowledge and human interests. Philosophy of the Social Sciences, 3,* 157–189.

Halliday, M. A. K. (1966, 1967, 1968). Notes on transitivity and theme in English. *Journal of Linguistics,* Part 1, *2,* 37–81; Part 2, *3,* 199–244; Part 3, *4,* 179–215.

Halliday, M. A.K. (1970). Language structure and language function. In J. Lyons (Ed.), *New Horizons in Linguistics.*

Halliday, M. A. K. (1973). *Explorations in the functions of language.* London: Edward Arnold.

Halliday, M. A. K., & Hasan, R. (1976). *Cohesion in English.* London: Longman.

Hauser, S. T. (1981). Physician-patient relationships. In E. G. Mishler, L. R. AmaraSingham, S. T. Hauser, R. Liem, S. D. Osherson, & N. E. Waxler, *Social contexts of health, illness, and patient care.* Cambridge: Cambridge University Press.

Howard, J., Davis, F., Pope, C., & Ruzek, S. (1977). Humanizing health care: The implications of technology, centralization, and self-care. *Medical Care* (Supplement), *15*(5), 11–26.

Hymes, D. (1971). Competence and performance in linguistic theory. In R. Huxley & E. Ingram (Eds.), *Language acquisition: Models and methods*. New York: Academic Press.

Jay, M. (1973). *The dialectical imagination: A history of the Frankfurt School and the Institute of Social Research, 1923-50*. Boston, MA: Little, Brown & Co.

Jefferson, G. (1972). Side sequences. In D. Sudnow (Ed.), *Studies in social interaction*. New York: Free Press.

Jefferson, G. (1978). Explanation of transcript notation. In J. Schenkein (Ed.), *Studies in the organization of conversational interaction*. New York: Academic Press.

Joos, M. (1961). *The five clocks*. New York: Harcourt, Brace and World.

Korsch, B. M., Gozzi, E. K., & Francis, V. (1968). Gaps in doctor-patient communication: 1. Doctor-patient interaction and patient satisfaction. *Pediatrics, 42*(5), 855–71.

Korsch, B. M., & Negrete, V. F. (1972). Doctor-patient communication. *Scientific American, 227*, 66–74.

Krause, E. A. (1977). *Power and illness: The political sociology of health and medical care*. New York: Elsevier.

Kress, G. (1976). *Halliday: System and function in language*. London: Oxford University Press.

Labov, W., & Fanshel, D. (1977). *Therapeutic discourse: Psychotherapy as conversation*. New York: Academic Press.

Lazare, A., & Eisenthal, S. (1977). Patient requests in a walk-in clinic. *Journal of Nervous and Mental Disease, 165*, 330–340.

Lazare, A., Eisenthal, S., & Wasserman, L. (1975). The customer approach to patienthood: Attending to patient requests in a walk-in clinic. *Archives of General Psychiatry, 32*, 553–558.

Lazare, A., Eisenthal, S., Wasserman, L., & Harford, T. C. (1975). Patient requests in a walk-in clinic. *Comprehensive Psychiatry, 16*, 467–477.

Lennard, H. L., & Bernstein, A. (1960). *The anatomy of psychotherapy: Systems of communication and expectation*. New York: Columbia University Press.

Lyons, J. (1970). *New horizons in linguistics*. Harmondsworth, England: Penguin Books.

McCarthy, T. (1978). *The critical theory of Jurgen Habermas*. Cambridge, MA: MIT Press.

Mechanic, D., & Levine, S. (1977). Issues in promoting health (Committee Reports of the Medical Sociology Section of the American Sociological Association). *Medical Care* (Supplement), *15*(5), 101 pgs. + x.

Millman, M. (1977). *The unkindest cut: Life in the backrooms of medicine*. New York: William Morrow.

Mishler, E. G. (1975a). Studies in dialogue and discourse: An exponential law of successive questioning. *Language in Society, 4*, 31–51.

Mishler, E. G. (1975b). Studies in dialogue and discourse: II. Types of discourse initiated by and sustained through questioning. *Journal of Psycholinguistic Research, 4*(2), 99–121.

Mishler, E. G. (1978). Studies in dialogue and discourse: III. Utterance structure and utterance function in interrogative sequences. *Journal of Psycholinguistic Research, 7*(4), 279–305.

Mishler, E. G. (1979a). Meaning in context: Is there any other kind? *Harvard Educational Review, 49*(1), 1–19.

Mishler, E. G. (1979b). *Discourse and meaning in medical interviews.* Research grant proposal submitted to the Medical Foundation, Inc. Unpublished.

Mishler, E. G. (1979c). Wou' you trade cookies with the popcorn? Talk of trades among six year olds. In O. K. Garnica & M. L. King (Eds.), *Language, children and society.* New York: Pergamon Press.

Mishler, E. G. (1981). Viewpoint: Critical perspectives on the biomedical model. In E. G. Mishler, L. R. AmaraSingham, S. T. Hauser, R. Liem, S. D. Osherson, & N. E. Waxler, *Social contexts of health, illness, and patient care.* Cambridge: Cambridge University Press.

Mishler, E. G., AmaraSingham, L. R., Hauser, S. T., Liem, R., Osherson, S., & Waxler, N. E. (1981). *Social contexts of health, illness, and patient care.* Cambridge: Cambridge University Press.

Mishler, E. G., & Waxler, N. E. (1968). *Interaction in families.* New York: Wiley.

Morrison, M. (1970). Compliance with medical requirements: A review of literature. *Nursing Research, 19,* 312–323.

Navarro, V. (1976). *Medicine under capitalism.* New York: Prodist.

Oxford University Dictionary. (3rd ed., Rev.) (1955). London: Oxford University Press.

Paget, M. A. (1978). *The unity of mistakes: A phenomenological study of medical work.* Unpublished doctoral dissertation, Michigan State University.

Paget, M. A. (1981a). The ontological anguish of women artists. *New England Sociologist, 3,* 65–79.

Paget, M. (1981b). *Phenomenological investigations of clinical silences.* Fellowship Application, National Endowment for the Humanities, Unpublished.

Paget, M. (1983a). On the work of talk: Studies in misunderstanding. In S. Fisher & A. Todd (Eds.), *The social organization of doctor-patient communication.* Washington, DC: Center for Applied Linguistics.

Paget, M. A. (1983b). Experience and knowledge. *Human Studies, 6,* 67–90.

Parsons, T. (1951). *The social system.* New York: Free Press.

Psathas, G. (1979). *Everyday language.* New York: Irvington.

Rochester, D., & Martin, J. R. (1979). *Crazy talk.* New York: Plenum.

Ruzek, S. B. (1978). *The women's health movement: Feminist alternatives to medical control.* New York: Praeger.

Sacks, H. (1972). On the analyzability of stories by children. In J. J. Gumperz & D. Hymes (Eds.), *Directions in sociolinguistics.* New York: Holt, Rinehart and Winston.

Sacks, H., Schegloff, E. A., & Jefferson, G. (1974). A simplest systematics for the organization of turn taking for conversation. *Language, 50*(4), 696–735.

Schegloff, E. A., Jefferson, G., & Sacks, H. (1977). The preference for self-correction in the organization of repair in conversation. *Language, 53*(2), 361–82.

Schenkein, J. (Ed.). (1978). *Studies in the organization of conversational interaction.* New York: Academic Press.

Schutz, A. (1962). *Collected papers, I. The problem of social reality.* The Hague: Martinus Nijhoff.

Shuy, R. (1974). Problems of communication in the cross-cultural medical interview. *Working Papers: Sociolinguistics #19.* Austin: University of Texas.

Shuy, R. (1976). The medical interview: Problems in communication. *Primary Care, 3*(3), 365–386.

Silverman, D., & Torode, B. (1980). *The material word.* London: Routledge & Kegan Paul.

Simon, A., & Boyer, E. G. (1970). *Mirrors for behavior, II* (Vols. A and B). Philadelphia, PA: Research for Better Schools.

Sinclair, J. Mch., & Coulthard, R. M. (1975). *Towards an analysis of discourse.* London: Oxford University Press.

Stanley, M. (1978). *The technological conscience: Survival and dignity in an age of expertise.* New York: Free Press, 1978. (Chicago: University of Chicago Press, Phoenix Edition, 1981).

Stimson, G. V. (1974). Obeying doctor's orders: A view from the other side. *Social Science and Medicine, 8,* 97–104.

Tinsley, H. E. A., & Weiss, D. J. (1975). Interrater reliability and agreement of subjective judgments. *Journal of Counseling Psychology, 1975, 22*(4), 358–376.

Waitzkin, H. (1978). *The informative process in medical care: Terminal progress report.* Unpublished.

Waitzkin, H., & Stoeckle, J. D. (1972). The communication of information about illness: Clinical, sociological, and methodological considerations. *Advances in Psychosomatic Medicine, 8,* 180–215.

Waitzkin, H., & Stoeckle, J. D. (1976). Information control and the micropolitics of health care: Summary of an ongoing research project. *Social Science and Medicine, 10,* 263–276.

Waitzkin, H., Stoeckle, J. D., Beller, E., & Mons, C. (1978). The informative process in medical care: A preliminary report with implications for instructional communication. *Instructional Science, 7,* 385–419.

Waitzkin, H., & Waterman, B. (1974). *The exploitation of illness in capitalist society*. Indianapolis, IN: Bobbs-Merrill.

Waterman, B., & Waitzkin, H. (1977). *Ideology and social control in the doctor-patient relationship*. Unpublished.

Waxler, N. E., & Mishler, E. G. (1966). Scoring and reliability problems in interaction process analysis: A methodological note. *Sociometry, 29*(1), 28–40.

Weick, K. E. (1968). Systematic observational methods. In G. Lindzey & E. Aronson (Eds.), *Handbook of social psychology* (2nd ed.) (Vol. 2). Reading, MA: Addison-Wesley Press.

Weiss, R. L. (1976). *Marital interaction coding system (MICS): Training and reference manual for coders*. Eugene: University of Oregon, Marital Studies Center.

Weiss, R. L., Hops, H., & Patterson, G. R. (1973). A framework for conceptualizing marital conflict, A technology for altering it, Some data for evaluating it. In F. W. Clark & L. A. Hammerlynck (Eds.), *Critical issues in research and practice: Proceedings of the fourth Banff international conference on behavior modification*. Champaign, IL: Research Press.

Wooton, A. (1975). *Dilemmas of discourse: Controversies about the sociological interpretation of language*. London: Allen & Unwin.

Yarrow, M. R., & Waxler, C. Z. (1979) Observing interaction: A confrontation with methodology. In R. B. Cairns (Ed.), *The analysis of social interactions: Methods, issues, and illustrations*. Hillsdale, NJ: Lawrence Erlbaum Associates.

Author Index

Italic page numbers indicate bibliographic citations.

Subject Index